PROBLEM LOAN STRATEGIES

John E. McKinley, III
Executive Vice President
The Citizens and Southern National Bank
Atlanta, Ga.

Ben F. Johnson, III
Partner
Alston & Bird
Atlanta, Ga.

Edward P. Vollertsen, III
Senior Vice President
e Citizens and Southern National Bank
Atlanta, Ga.

R. Neal Batson
Partner
Alston & Bird
Atlanta, Ga.

John C. Weitnauer
Partner
Alston & Bird
Atlanta, Ga.

ROBERT MORRIS ASSOCIATES

The National Association of Bank Loan and Credit Officers
Philadelphia, Pennsylvania

About Robert Morris Associates

Robert Morris Associates (RMA) is the national association of bank loan and credit officers. Founded in 1914, RMA has grown to over 2,800 banks which represent 90% of all U.S. commercial banking resources. These banks are represented in the association by more than 11,500 commercial loan and credit officers and related personnel in all 50 states, Puerto Rico, Canada, and several offshore cities.

RMA was named after the American patriot who signed the Declaration of Independence, who was largely responsible for the financing of our Revolutionary War, and who helped establish our banking system.

The association's original purpose back in 1914 was to facilitate the flow and interchange of credit information. Today, this purpose has been expanded to include working continuously to improve the principles and practices of commercial lending, loan administration, and asset management in commercial banks.

RMA seeks to meet its objectives through educational services, regular publications such as *The Journal of Commercial Bank Lending*, and special publications such as this one.

Copyright© 1985 by Robert Morris Associates
All rights reserved. Printed in the U.S.A.
Library of Congress Catalog Card Number: 84-27222
International Standard Book Number: 0-936742-20-8

Library of Congress Cataloging in Publication Data
Main entry under title:

Problem loan strategies.

Includes index.
1. Bank loans. I. McKinley, John E.
HG1641.P78 1985   332.1'753'0685   84-27222
ISBN 0-936742-20-8

Additional copies of this publication are available from the Order Department, Robert Morris Associates, 1616 Philadelphia National Bank Building, Philadelphia, PA 19107 (215)665-2850.

Table of Contents

Foreword

Robert Morris Associates (RMA) is committed to providing programs, products, and services that enhance the professional expertise of commercial loan and credit officers. While no one intends to make problem loans, most banks do anticipate having problem loans and loan losses as a cost of doing business. Problem loans are a fact of life. Accordingly, it is our intent to provide a tool that assists bankers in handling problem loans.

It is the philosophy of this publication that problem loans can be treated as an informed decision process which minimizes the loss to the bank. This process begins with prevention, continues through detection, and eventually reaches a solution. The solution is the course of action that will result in the greatest benefit to the bank.

The chart on page 8 illustrates this philosophy and also parallels the content of each chapter

Summary of the Chapters

When dealing with problem loans, the process begins with *prevention*. Chapter 1 discusses those basics of sound banking and portfolio management which must be adhered to if excessive problem loans and losses are to be avoided.

Even the best-managed banks expect a reasonable level of problems. Consequently, we must be able to rely on early *detection* as the second line of defense against problem loans. Early detection requires several elements—good loan underwriting, a well-trained account officer, and good credit administration. Each of these elements is addressed in Chapter 2.

Once a potential problem loan has been identified, *gathering information* should proceed immediately. Chapter 3 deals with the basic information that is useful in most situations and the sources to be tapped to assist the information-gathering process. Only with reliable information can we properly analyze the problem.

As the problem loan process continues, we advance now to the *analysis* phase. Chapter 4 discusses how management analysis determines if management is capable of correcting the problem and how financial analysis determines root causes and possible solutions. Through analysis, the

Decision Process for Problem Loans

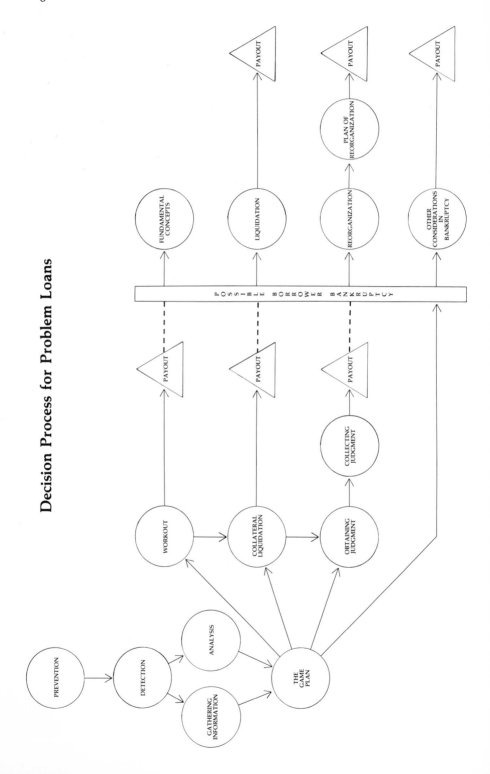

puzzle begins to take sufficient shape to allow some conclusions to be drawn about possible solutions.

Based upon the information gathered and the analysis of the problem loan, the banker begins *developing the game plan*. Chapter 5 provides several available options. The banker must develop with the attorney a plan that is feasible and takes into account the various actions and reactions of the borrower and other creditors. The ultimate goal of the game plan is to get the bank's money back.

One option is *workout*. Workout is defined as the cooperative, voluntary agreement between bank and borrower to establish a framework for the repayment of indebtedness. Chapter 6 covers the purpose and problems of workout.

Often the most direct route from credit discomfort to payout is through *liquidating the collateral*. It is the fortunate banker who find his or her loan sufficiently collateralized to make it unnecessary to consider any other problem loan solution. Chapter 7 addresses collateral liquidation on a strategic basis, looking at the entire collateral package and determining an overall liquidation plan.

Some problem loans are best handled when the lender decides on *reducing the debt to judgment*. A judgment evidences a court decision that settles the respective rights and claims of the lender and the borrower. Chapter 8 discusses the growing number of potential borrower issues which the lender may have to hurdle to obtain judgment.

Having obtained a judgment, the banker must still deal with *collecting the judgment*. Chapter 9 expands on some of the weapons which the judgment makes available to the lender. These include discovery, levy, garnishment, and receivership.

The final option for the banker may be *bankruptcy*. Chapter 10 provides a grounding in basic bankruptcy law and procedures. This understanding will assist the banker in evaluating the strength of the borrower's negotiating position and also improves communication between the banker and counsel.

Chapter 11 continues the discussion of bankruptcy by focusing on *liquidation cases*. Typically, in a Chapter 7 (liquidation) bankruptcy, the banker is concerned only with getting the collateral away from the clutches of the bankruptcy court. There are basically two ways to do this. One is to obtain an abandonment from the trustee. The other is to seek relief from the automatic stay.

In contrast to the typical Chapter 7 case, a Chapter 11 (reorganization) case can present many different issues and many more complex matters of strategy. The goal of a Chapter 11 debtor is to propose and have confirmed a plan of reorganization which extends the time needed to pay the debts and/or reduce the amount of some of those debts as well. The goal of the creditors, in contrast, is to get paid as much as possible as soon as possible. Our discussion of *reorganization cases* begins in Chapter 12 and develops into a *plan of reorganization* in Chapter 13.

Chapter 14 completes our discussion of bankruptcy by covering such *other considerations* as involuntary bankruptcies and cases concerning individuals.

In summary, this publication seeks to address the handling of problem loans as a process: a process that requires decisions, strategies, and patience; a process that requires in-depth information, detailed planning, and good counsel; a process that results in the greatest benefit to the bank.

About the Authors

John E. McKinley, III. John is an executive vice president at The Citizens & Southern National Bank, Atlanta, where he is the bank's senior credit officer. He received his B.A. from Davidson College and his M.B.A. from the University of North Carolina. His banking background includes experience in international and corporate lending, as well as branch management and credit administration. John is a contributing author to the RMA/ABA *Loan Officer Development Seminar* and is on the faculty of the Stonier Graduate School of Banking and the RMA Uniform Credit Analysis Seminar. John is the author of Chapters 1–4.

Ben F. Johnson, III. Ben in a partner in the law firm of Alston & Bird, Atlanta, where he specializes in banking-related litigation and regulatory work. He received his B.A. degree from Emory University and his J.D. from Harvard. Ben is a lecturer in problem loans and workouts at Stonier and has written numerous *Law Review* articles concerning practice and procedure. Ben is a contributing author for Chapters 5–9.

Edward P. Vollersten, III. Ed is a senior vice president at The Citizens & Southern National Bank, Atlanta, where he now serves as senior credit officer for the capital markets and treasury group, C&S Georgia Corp. He received his B.A. from Yale University and his M.B.A. from Georgia State University. Ed has spent the past 14 years principally in credit administration and workouts, having headed up C&S's workout division for two years. He also serves on the faculty of the Stonier Graduate School of Banking. Ed is a contributing author for Chapters 5–9.

R. Neal Batson. Neal is a partner in the law firm of Alston & Bird, Atlanta, where he serves as chairman of the Litigation Department. He received his J.D. in 1966 from Vanderbilt University School of Law. Neal is a former law clerk to the Honorable Griffin B. Bell and a past president of the Atlanta Bar Association. A former adjunct professor at Emory University School of Law, Neal lectures frequently on trial tactics. Neal is a contributing author for Chapters 10–14.

John C. Weitnauer. Kit is a partner in the law firm of Alston & Bird, Atlanta, where he specializes in creditors' rights and bankruptcy. He received his J.D. *cum laude* in 1977 from the University of Georgia School of Law and is a frequent author and lecturer on bankruptcy practices and trends. Kit is a contributing author for Chapters 10–14.

Acknowledgments

RMA wishes to recognize Richard H. Daniel, executive vice president, Security Pacific National Bank, and R. Edwin Spears, senior vice president, North Carolina National Bank, for their work in reviewing the original manuscript. Special appreciation is also given to the members of the 1983-84 Domestic Lending Division Council.

RMA and the authors also acknowledge all those bankers and borrowers whose experiences and efforts made this publication possible.

Domestic Lending Division
Robert Morris Associates
Philadelphia, Pennsylvania

Preventing Problem Loans 1

A problem loan is one which cannot be paid according to terms or in a satisfactory manner. It will bear risk which is high in proportion to return and there may be probability of loss.

The handling of a problem loan requires special attention and expertise. A complex problem can be in the workout process for months or even years and can require the involvement of bankers, lawyers, certified public accountants (CPAs), consultants, and other specialists. The workout process can also be expensive and difficult, and the bank with too many problems in its portfolio can be crippled by the costs associated with workout, charge-off, and lost opportunity. The best approach is to establish a lending program that incorporates all the elements of prevention.

Four Ps of Prevention

All banks anticipate having problem loans and loan losses as a cost of doing business. However, there are basics of sound banking and portfolio management which must be adhered to if excessive problem loans and losses are to be avoided. Although it is beyond the scope of this book to cover all aspects of loan administration, it is useful to consider in general terms the four "Ps" of problem loan prevention.

Philosophy

A bank's lending environment is established by the philosophy which is communicated by top management to its lenders. For example, a bank which pursues a higher risk, higher return, or an aggressive growth philosophy encourages a potentially dangerous lending attitude. Emphasis on growth or return often comes at the expense of credit quality as lenders are pushed to meet the bank's objectives.

An analysis of problem banks in the recent past would indicate that despite good basic credit procedures, major problem situations are encountered when:

- Banks have ventured too aggressively into a new lending field without adequate experience or expertise.
- An overly aggressive lending posture has been pursued with heavy emphasis on loan production.

13

The idea that problem loan prevention is the sole providence of credit administration or even of the lending areas is erroneous. Preventing problem loan starts at the very top of the organization and depends equally on the lending culture that is created and the strategic decisions of management.

Management communicates its philosophy not only by a direct expression of its desire for quality loans and limited loan losses but also by setting specific goals for past dues, loan losses, and criticized and classified loans and by managing these goals effectively. If accomplishment of goals is constantly encouraged and recognized, it becomes a priority. If the goals are only paid lip service by management, they will be ignored or forgotten by the lenders.

Policy

The bank's policy embodies management's instructions which are designed to guide lenders to follow the general lending philosophy. The lending policy is the primary means of communicating the bank's lending philosophy. It outlines the bank's definition of sound lending practices and the loan approval and review procedures. For the policy to be effective, there must be a commitment by management to administer it actively. It must be easily understood, rigidly adhered to, and well communicated.

Policies fail which are:

- Not adhered to—there is not sufficient commitment by management to ensure enforcement.
- Poorly communicated—the policy may be well thought out and thorough, but the lenders don't understand it or know how to use it.
- Poorly conceived, inadequate, poorly organized, or written.
- Undermined by the bank's informal or unwritten policy.

Account officers are guided by signals from the organization which indicate the bank's true priorities. For example, if top management emphasizes and rewards production at the expense of credit quality, the account officer will respond accordingly. If top management lends as if there were no policy or fails to require strict adherence, signals are provided which can undermine the written policy and result in overaggressive lending or sloppy credit practices.

Procedures

Procedures consist of the systems and controls which assure that policy exceptions are brought to management's attention. It includes loan approval and review procedures, loan rating systems, and systems to provide management-type information on the portfolio. This is the second line of defense in recognizing a developing problem loan—the loan officer is the first. Without effective procedures, lending practices can deteriorate, perhaps gradually without being detected.

People

The loan officer is the first line of defense in preventing and recognizing problem loans. If good loan decisions are made in accordance with the lending policy, are thoroughly analyzed, and well documented, many problem loans can be avoided. However, problems will develop for reasons beyond the control of the bank. The loan officer is the primary customer contact and should be the first to detect the symptoms and take the appropriate action. To ensure that the loan officer has the capability to prevent and recognize problems, the bank must hire and train well-qualified people and staff the lending areas adequately.

Just as a bank should not outgrow its equity base, neither should it outgrow its personnel base. When allocating human resources, the tendency is to allocate first to the line and then send to staff whatever is left. This practice can undermine the effectiveness of credit administration. Not only are there less qualified people in the credit areas but an attitude is created which ensures that the best people will not want to be assigned to credit administration. They perceive that their authority or importance is subordinated to the line. Proper staffing of credit administration should start at the top where a capable and respected person should be given authority to do the assigned task.

If all the elements of prevention are present, loan officers will be lending exactly as management would if it were making all the loans. Practices will conform with policy, and the bank's general portfolio trends will reflect the desired results.

Costs of Problem Loans

The costs associated with problem loans are far greater than loan loss figures would indicate. There are indirect costs which are not always evident or easily calculated but which can become an important factor in setting workout strategy. Some of these indirect costs are discussed below.

Legal Expenses

Because of the complexity of bankruptcy law and the often protracted nature of workouts, legal expense can be a major consideration in determining workout strategy. There have been cases, not infrequently, where banks would have maximized return by accepting an early settlement at a deep discount. However, by the time that litigation was final and eventual settlement rendered, the bank's net recovery was actually smaller because of attorneys' fees.

Despite the potential high legal expense often associated with work-out, it is a mistake to accept poor quality legal advice. Even though good legal counsel can be expensive, the cost pales in comparison with the risk of becoming an "insider" or a "control" party and losing the entire loan or assuming all the borrower's liabilities.

If a bitter and drawn out legal battle is anticipated, the banker should request an initial fee estimate describing the scope of the work and the time and expense involved. As the case progresses, the estimate should be updated. With this input, a strategy can be devised to maximize the bank's net return.

Administrative Expense

The decision to workout a problem loan on the assumption that the bank will never lose a penny of its principal may be based on erroneous logic. Although there will be no loan loss, it is virtually impossible to achieve a reasonable return on a problem loan because of the administrative costs.

A problem loan requires far more administration and attention than a fully performing loan. This time is basically nonproductive and could be better spent generating revenue rather than preserving principal. Not only are large chunks of the account officer's time devoted to working with the borrower but there are also added audit and review requirements. Additional reports must be prepared and more frequent update reviews needed, which in turn ties up the time of senior management and credit administrators. In addition, there possibly are expenses for outside specialists such as CPAs, appraisers, and consultants. If problems become excessive, there are additional costs from special credit and audit committees of the board of directors. Fees from outside auditors also escalate, as the loan portfolio and loss reserve are more closely scrutinized.

Although administrative costs are difficult to quantify, the bank with a large portfolio of problem loans can anticipate a dramatic impact on profitability. If loan yields were calculated on the assumption of much higher risk in the portfolio, the combined effects of increased funding costs (as the result of lower paper/bond ratings), increased cost of risk, and increased administrative overhead result in a very poor yield for the loan portfolio.

Reputation

The cost of a damaged reputation may be one of the highest costs associated with problem loans. A bank, more than most businesses, lives on its reputation. If as a result of excessive loan problems, a bank's reputation is damaged in the eyes of its customers, its funds providers, the investment community, and the general banking community, not only may the bank lose existing customers and the opportunity to gain valuable new customers but its cost of funds may rise and its stock price may fall. If the bank must increase capital, it may find the cost of capital extremely high, if available at all. With a sullied reputation, the bank may find it is neither an attractive acquiror nor acquiree candidate and that it is unable to take advantage of market opportunities.

Regulatory Expenses

Any bank president or board of directors who has operated under a letter agreement, "consent and undertaking," or any other such arrangement with either a bank regulatory authority or the Securities and Exchange Commission can appreciate the expenses associated with such an arrangement. There may be expenses to set up special committees of the board of directors to approve loans of certain sizes and types. There may be special audit committees to whom the credit review and audit functions report. Furthermore, the bank may find itself filing regular special reports with banking regulators, giving specific plans of actions and results of those plans on criticized credit over certain sizes. Special approval of the board of directors may be required to advance new money or to renew lines to criticized borrowers.

Not only is there expense associated with such requirements but management may lose control of the bank to others. This makes for an extended decision-making process, where the decision as to what is in the best interest of the bank is influenced, if not made, by someone other than management. Furthermore, actual time delays in getting requisite approvals may cause good banking opportunities to be lost. At a minimum, the bank experiences a great loss of momentum. The lenders may become reluctant to bring in new business or to accept even a normal risk. The bank then finds it difficult to book enough loans at high enough rates to restore earnings and to overcome the earnings drag from the nonaccruing assets. Thus, the problems tend to perpetuate themselves.

Personnel Expense

A bank that is encountering extensive loan difficulties frequently loses its best people because they cannot anticipate large salary increases or bonuses in the near term. Moreover, they may see their long-term career prospects jeopardized by association with a "problem" bank. Facing the possibility of losing its best people when they are needed most, the bank must hire new people and pay a premium to attract them.

The earnings pressures associated with excessive problem loans often result in expense controls and hiring freezes. There may be a cessation or a severe cut back in the hiring of management associates, and the bank finds itself understaffed when conditions improve. The temptation then is to hire new management associates and put them on the line too soon, risking poor loan decisions because of inexperienced lenders.

Borrowing Expense

When a bank is perceived as having an excessive number of problem loans, the marketplace will charge the bank more for funds due to the increased risk. If the bank's status is perceived to be *too* risky, it will find itself shut out of all money markets, except for the Fed window, the lender of last resort. As a result, profitability and growth are hampered making it harder to build equity or raise capital. With this handicap, the return to competitiveness and sound financial strength can be long and hard.

Lost Opportunity

Opportunities for normal growth and expansion are beyond the grasp of the organization which finds itself struggling with excessive loan problems. This could be the overriding theme associated with the costs of problem loans. Some banks find the costs so steep that their very existence are endangered. But for the majority of banks, opportunities are lost as the result of the factors mentioned—strenuous supervision by regulatory agencies, inadequate financial resources, damaged reputation, and inadequate staffing. The competitive disadvantages associated with excessive problem loans can be so significant that a bank's status in the marketplace is permanently altered.

In summary, all these costs hurt the bank in a myriad of subtle and not so subtle ways. One is reminded of a form of torture and death known as the "death of a thousand cuts" seen in the American Southwest among the native Americans. The captive dies by slowly bleeding to death from many small nicks inflicted upon him by the women and children. No one cut is enough by itself to kill him, but the cumulative effect of all the small cuts eventually does.

In many ways, it is like that for a bank with enough problem loans so that it is perceived as a problem bank. The bank bleeds from all these small cuts and has a very hard, slow time recovering from the problems. In the meantime, the officers, employees, and shareholders all suffer.

Should Your Bank Have a Workout Function?

Problem loan workouts should be administered by experienced lenders who can provide objectivity. Workout is a highly specialized and time-consuming task which requires skills not possessed by many account officers. Consequently, most banks could benefit from the existence of a workout area with specialists available to handle problem loans. However, the individual bank's size and objectives should determine the organization and role of the workout function.

Auxiliary Function

A small bank with limited problems might simply assign the workout responsibility to a credit person or lender as an auxiliary function. This person would be responsible for staying abreast of such legal developments as changes in bankruptcy law and maintaining contacts with legal counsel, business brokers or auctioneers, appraisers, consultants, CPAs, and others who would be helpful in a workout situation. He or she might or might not handle workouts personally but would at least provide direction and supervision to the process. If required to handle workouts personally, the banker must have flexibility to adapt to periods when the workouts will dominate his or her schedule since a complex workout can be quite time-consuming.

Specific Department

At the other extreme, the bank has all workouts in a department specifically designated for that purpose. This department generally is staffed with specialists, possibly including lawyers, or lenders with a legal background and good analytical and negotiating skills. The advantage of this arrangement is that account officers are free to develop business and service customers and it ensures that the two key ingredients for successful workouts are present: expertise and objectivity. What may be lost is the account officer's knowledge of, and working relationship with, the customer and the value of the learning experience for the account officer.

Banks with large problem portfolios, especially those concentrated in a specific industry or bank department, especially benefit from a department to which workouts can be transferred. This allows the originating department or area of the bank to continue to function somewhat normally. In banks with problems concentrated in one industry, such as the energy industry, a workout area can be organized within the lending area and staffed by energy specialists *and* workout specialists.

Alternative Approaches

Many banks strike a happy medium between these alternatives. They maintain a workout function, usually within the credit administration area but limit the scope. Instead of handling the majority of workouts, the workout function acts as consultants in the analysis of the problem, the development of the workout plan, and the determination of who should handle the credit. It also monitors the progress of the workout process through reports and direct contact.

Often, the account officer continues to handle the credit with participation or supervision from an area credit officer. This can be effective in banks with decentralized credit organizations where credit officers are attached to the line lending functions. The determination to move the credit to the workout area is based on the complexity of the problem and time required to administer, the availability of an account officer with the necessary experience and objectivity to handle it, and the likelihood of restoring the company's health and desirability as a customer.

In summary, the key to successful loan workouts is the ability of the bank to bring the necessary expertise and objectivity to the process. Workout is one of the most specialized of a bank's lending functions and requires skills that cannot usually be found in most account officers. It requires the ability to move quickly and to make important decisions based on an understanding of commercial and bankruptcy law which is complex and regularly changes with new precedents. It requires the ability to make intelligent compromises and it can be time-consuming, especially for the inexperienced.

Although a good lawyer can be helpful, workout requires good business judgment, the ability to read people and negotiate toughly, the ability to analyze problems and draw conclusions, and the patience to see the workout process through. It can mean working with lawyers, customers, consultants, and the courts for months. Any bank that has a normal portfolio of problem loans needs to develop the specialized expertise needed to administer that portfolio.

Who Should Handle the Workout

As mentioned, the workout must involve a banker with objectivity and expertise. The assessment of his or her qualifications should be made by someone with sufficient workout experience, usually someone from the workout or credit administration areas, possibly in conjunction with line management.

Objectivity and Expertise

If the account officer has a close personal relationship with the officers of the company, if the account officer made the initial loan decision, or if the account officer has been slow to react to obvious warning signs, his or her objectivity should be questioned.

The complexity of the credit and the lending and previous workout experience of the account officer should make the expertise issue easier to settle. Additional factors include the account officer's mental toughness, negotiating skills, demonstrated ability to identify the problem and deal with it effectively so far, and analytical capabilities.

Other considerations in the decision of who should handle the credit include:

- Time required to administer the workout. How will this affect the account officer's ability to service other customers?

- Value of the learning experience.
- Is the account officer's knowledge of the customer and working relationship invaluable to the workout?
- Having a "hatchet man" come into the picture from another area of the bank. If the account officer must foreclose a member in good standing of the community, will it undermine the account officer's relations with other members of the community?
- Ability to restore the credit and retain the customer on a friendly basis.
- Possibly strained relations if the customer is moved to a workout area.

The decision may not simply be to move the account to a workout area or leave it with the account officer. If the account officer is only partially deficient in the needed skills, he or she can be involved with all decisions made by a credit person, line supervisor, or the workout specialist. The account officer would be responsible for carrying out the bank's plan but would not have final authority. The objectivity and expertise could be provided initially by another party until the account officer can act independently.

Another alternative would be to keep the credit within the area where industry and banking expertise resides but move it to a more experienced and objective account officer. Because the question of who handles the workout is so crucial to the issues of expertise and objectivity, it is one of the most important decisions involved in the workout process.

Legal Counsel

There is an additional issue which does not directly relate to the account officer. That is the question of legal counsel. Just as workout is a specialized lending function, it is also a highly specialized legal function. Even good commercial lending counsel cannot be relied on for expert workout advice. The lawyer should be as much a workout specialist as the banker, and the bank should develop a relationship and rapport between workout specialists in the bank and the law firm. Those banks which have legal counsel within the workout area are assured of the availability of legal workout expertise. But banks with in-house counsel whose experience in workouts is limited may need to look to outside counsel in complex workouts.

The Problem Bank

When the bank's list of problem loans has grown beyond acceptable levels and the general quality of the portfolio cannot meet industry standards, bank management must review its general lending practices and find an effective means to prevent new problems while dealing with already existing ones. Prevention of new problems entails a return to basics, that is, those factors detailed in the four Ps of prevention. More specifically, the credit administration function must be closely reviewed and strengthened. Existing problems must be vigorously attacked, either by establishing a workout area or by providing added emphasis to an existing area.

Strengthening Credit Administration

•Start at the top. The manager of credit administration should have the capacity and authority to get the job done and should have his or her mission clearly focused. In other words, credit administration should be managed by a person of stature whose capabilities and authority equal those of line management peers. Credit administration should be his or her first and foremost priority. It should not be a responsibility which was added on to lending or other responsibilities. Without the kind of person who enjoys the respect of the line and who has equal authority with the management of the lending function, the prospects of improving the bank's lending procedures are limited.

•Review the lending policy. Does it provide clear and concise guidance to the line? Is it being communicated and followed? What controls are in place to assure that violations or exceptions are noticed?

•Review the bank's lending authorities. Are they too liberal? Are they being adhered to? Is the loan approval process effective and is there accountability at all approval levels?

•Review the loan grading system. Is it easily understood or are categories too broad or poorly defined? Will it help identify developing problems? Is it being used effectively by the lenders and by management? Is it clear who is responsible for establishing the grade?

•Evaluate the loan review function. Is this area getting the priority it deserves in terms of the management and staff that are provided? Or is it regarded as a convenient dumping ground for account officers who can't cut it? Does it receive management support and backing so that it has both the resources and authority to be effective?

•Determine if account officers are adequately trained and supervised. Are they encouraged to seek help? Is the importance of training emphasized in performance evaluations? Is job performance measured against standards and goals? Is accountability clearly established and rewarded?

These are steps which should be taken whenever a bank suffers from excessive loan losses as a result of poor lending practices. Obviously, this won't solve the problem if the bank has aggressively entered a new field where there is limited in-bank expertise available or where management philosophy is contrary to conservative lending practices.

The Workout Function

If the bank already has a workout area, the addition of a large volume of problems may mean that previous management and staffing are no longer adequate. The manager of the area cannot simply be the most senior member of the staff or necessarily the best workout specialist in the bank. New management may be necessary—a manager who has the ability to attract, motivate, and manage the new account officers which will be needed in the area. He or she must also have the ability to communicate with the bank's top management and to enlist its support. For the area to be effective, it must have the authority and priority to make unpopular decisions, such as foreclosing on old customers.

The necessity for the workout area to possess independent authority is underlined by the difference in priorities of the line lending units and the workout area. Where the line might be concerned with loss of an old and valued customer and the deposit balances and revenues associated with the relationship, the workout area concerns itself primarily with the most expedient solution to a loan problem. Although the customer's interests must be considered, excessive loan problems may represent unacceptable costs to the bank. When this point is reached, the bank's workout posture must be adjusted so that decisive action can be assured.

Summary

The time to handle problem loans is before they go on the books. The costs associated with loan workouts and losses can undermine a bank's corporate presence—its market position, long-range market strategy, and reputation.

When a problem develops, the bank must have someone available with specialized workout skills and experience. If there are numerous problems, there should be a workout area where problems can be housed for special attention. In addition, the bank must act to eliminate the conditions which cause or allow problems to exist.

Detecting
Problem Loans 2

In the subtle art of loan portfolio management, there's a trade-off between prevention of problem loans and optimization of market opportunity. Even the best managed banks expect a "reasonable" level of problems. Consequently, they must be able to rely on early detection as an important part of their defense against problem loans.

Emphasis should be placed on the word "early," since the earlier the recognition, the greater the options available in workout. Banks that rely on systems such as past dues, overdrafts, and other exceptions as warning signs of a developing problem may find that the company's cash crisis has reached the advanced stages before these signs are detected. By the time overdrafts and past dues appear, management has taken means to preserve or generate cash and to avoid a cash crisis. These measures, though appropriate from the company's standpoint, may have prejudiced the bank's position and may, in fact, have hampered the workout process.

Profile of the Troubled Company

The source of a company's problems may be external, internal, or a combination. External includes such factors as the economy, competition, the environment, and government regulation. Internal includes management-related factors, financial structure, expense controls, marketing, production, and so on. Whatever the source, if the problem continues unresolved, it will produce repercussions and eventually result in a cash crisis. As an example, if there is an increase in competition and sales decline, a decrease in profitability may result. This reduced profitability could initiate a chain of events such as reduced capital spending, employee layoffs, reduced R&D expense, sell-off of assets, and eventually an inability to fund growth or repay debt.

As the chain progresses from the initial cause to a "cash crisis," signals are given that if detected early and analyzed can lead to corrective actions. These steps can interrupt the chain and avoid the cash crisis and problem loan workout situation. The particular characteristics of a chain of events leading to a cash crisis vary depending on the causes and management's reaction. However, a predictable pattern emerges in management's allocation of financial resources when a company begins experiencing financial difficulties.

Stages of a Cash Crisis

Stage 1—Cash Concern. Liquidity becoming strained. Management makes cash management a priority.

- Expenses reduced; salaries cut or raises delayed or reduced; bonuses cut or eliminated; overhead controls initiated; R&D curtailed.
- Asset management improved; accounts receivable collection efforts strengthened; inventory levels reduced; trade payments slowed.
- Capital expenditures reduced.
- Prices cut to move stale inventory.

Stage 2—Cash Crunch. Cash management becomes top priority. Management must generate sufficient amounts of cash to continue operations on a normal basis.

- Expenses further reduced.
- Capital expenditures eliminated.
- Perks reduced—pension, profit-sharing.
- Employee layoffs.
- Morale declines.
- Possible plant closings or elimination of nonprofitable lines.
- Nonessential assets sold.
- Salaries and bonuses accrued—not paid.
- Some creditors partially paid, some not at all, trade creditors stretched further, accounts payable become not payable.
- Company seeks additional borrowings or restructure of existing debt.
- New credit sources are sought.
- Assets are refinanced.
- Product quality suffers and returns and allowances increase.
- Maintenance of machinery and equipment suffers.
- Company seeks to hire new financial management or brings in financial consultant to improve systems.
- Dividends cut.
- Covenants of loan agreement violated.

Stage 3—Cash Crises. Company in do or die situation. Must take drastic measures to ensure survival.

- Additional assets sold.
- Layoffs continue—now includes officers.
- Morale hits rock bottom.
- Key employees resign.
- Perks eliminated—pensions, conventions, etc.

- Plants closed, subsidiaries sold.
- Change in top management.
- Overdrafts.
- Loans past due.
- Seasonal loans not paid out.
- Loan covenants violated and default becomes inevitable.
- Dividends eliminated.
- Taxes not paid.

Although the stages listed could vary considerably from case to case, several conclusions are possible. First, the banker may be one of the last parties to be directly affected by the company's problems. Overdrafts and past dues usually do not occur until other creditors have suffered and other emergency means have been taken. Available financial resources may have been diverted to suppliers or creditors in response to pressure, rather than being used to finance a constructive workout plan.

Consequently, the bank finds that parties whose interest were subordinate in liquidation have been paid from the proceeds of assets that were pledged to the bank as collateral. The very resources needed to finance a workout have been dissipated, and the remaining alternatives are liquidation of the company, bankruptcy, or additional bank debt to finance the workout—all unattractive alternatives.

This might be characterized as the steps most likely to be taken by a responsive management. The poorly managed company may march blithely past most of the steps in Stages 1 and 2. Instead, it will advance rapidly to Stage 3 and its probable financial demise.

This example certainly does not fit all situations in which companies face financial difficulties, but the elements are realistic and serve to illustrate the importance of early detection. It also leads to the conclusion that the tendency of bankers to act only after they are directly affected may be detrimental to their interests. It is not surprising that bankers sometimes develop a reputation for heavy handedness in problem loans. If no action is taken until the bank is affected, then closing down and liquidating may be the best or only remaining options.

From our example, it is clear that past dues and overdrafts are, in fact, late warning signs and that *early* detection depends on recognition of symptoms in the earliest stages. The only realistic method of early recognition is action by the account officer in coordination with prudent loan underwriting and effective credit administration.

Early Detection

All elements of problem loan detection are important, but the account officer is by far the most important. Recognition in the early stages is possible only if the account officer is diligent in the administration of loan relationships, communicates well with the borrower, and has a thorough knowledge of the borrower and his or her business.

The Account Officer

Early problem detection should result from recognition by the account officer that the borrower has deviated from established norms. These norms could be in three areas.

1. <u>Financial</u>

- Performance compared with plans.
- Performance compared with trends.
- Performance compared with peer companies in the same industry.
- Financial structure.

2. <u>Nonfinancial</u>

- Change in product mix.
- Change in market strategy.
- Rapid expansion plans.
- Management turnover or shuffling.
- Change in CPAs.
- Change in structure of board of directors.

3. <u>Personal</u>

- Lifestyle
- Personal investments.
- Personal behavior.
- Relationship with banker, CPA, etc.
- Willingness to provide information.

To know these norms and to recognize a deviation, the account officer must have the opportunity, as well as priority by bank management, to develop this depth of rapport, understanding, and communication. The account officer must maintain close contact with the borrower through plant visits and frequent communication and must develop a knowledge of the industry through industry contacts, trade journals, and the like. By becoming knowledgeable of the borrower's operation and industry, the account officer can become a more trusted advisor with whom the borrower will be more open and frank about developing problems, major policy decisions, and management changes. This represents the ideal environment for early problem loan recognition.

Credit Administration

The primary role of credit administration in early detection is to provide an environment which encourages the account officer to bring potentially developing problems to the attention of the bank and to seek help.

This assistance is usually in the form of analysis of the problem and development of the plan for handling it. Credit administration must be able to provide the specialized skills to assist the account officer but in a nonpunitive manner.

Credit administration must remain constantly alert for developing areas of concern, for example, deregulated industries, economically depressed areas or industries, industries affected by changes in government regulations or environmental factors. When an area is identified, policies and actions must be formulated and rapidly put into effect.

Finally, the importance of systems such as loan grading and exception reporting should not be overlooked. Although not capable of providing warnings on as timely a basis as desired, these systems provide an important backstop in the not unusual event that early warning symptoms are missed or ignored.

Loan Underwriting

Underwriting means the analysis, structuring, and documentation of the loan. The basis for communications is often established in the initial loan negotiation and structuring. Therefore, it is often the skill with which the loan is underwritten that ensures the account officer is capable of recognizing deviations from norms. Also, by proper underwriting, problem loan complications such as documentation errors are avoided.

Good underwriting begins with *analysis*—to determine the company's financial needs and repayment capacity. Also, analysis determines the "key control factors" of the business: those factors which are crucial to a particular business' success. From these factors are derived some of the norms which the account officer monitors in the administration of the loan. Poor analysis can result in poor loan structuring and an inability to properly monitor the loan after it is booked.

Loan *structuring* provides a means of control over the allocation of the company's cash resources. The tighter the terms, the less discretion management has since loan repayments place heavy demands on cash resources. If terms are too lenient, cash is available for other uses and loans become past due only after a severe cash problem exists. A properly structured loan does not place undue hardship on the borrower but is stringent enough to create past dues that warn of a problem rather than disclose the problem after it has fully developed.

In *documenting* the loan, the bank and borrower are establishing contractual agreements as to the obligations of each party and in the process determine their expectations about the nature of the relationship. In structuring the loan agreement, the bank attempts to ensure that information about the borrower will be forthcoming on a regular basis. If key control factors have been identified, information pertaining to them will be required. A well-executed agreement establishes a sound basis for future communication. A poorly executed document can hinder communications and bind the bank to its underwriting mistakes.

If notes, security agreements, and financing statements are poorly drawn or incomplete, collateral may be lost or costly litigation may result.

Major Causes of Problems

Although the list of possible causes for loan problems could fill a text, there are several major categories which account for the majority of problems. It is not unusual for a company's problems to include several causes, and often it is this pyramiding of causes that breaks the company's back. An understanding of these possible causes and knowledge of the profile of a troubled company provide the account officer with the background to recognize potential problems and the ability to select the best methods of dealing with them.

Not included in the following list of major causes are the actions of the account officer in contributing to the development of a problem loan situation. By overlending or improper loan structuring, the account officer can place undue financial strain on the company's financial resources. By failing to document or collateralize properly, the risk of loss to the bank is increased. By inadequate administration, the problem may be detected too late for effective action. When these shortcomings by the banker are combined with the following major causes of problems, the chances of a successful workout are diminished.

Management

Management has long been acknowledged as the primary cause of business failure. The definition of management as a cause is not limited to incompetence but covers a wide range of possibilities including inadequate depth, weakness in one or more major areas, failure of management to grow apace with the corporation, fraud, and embezzlement. The following list covers some of the most commonly encountered management shortcomings and suggests possible solutions.

Management needs have outgrown existing management capacity. Many companies are started by able salesmen or engineers or other technically skilled people who do not possess the general management skills needed for top management of large corporations. Management does not have the specialized skills needed to supervise various functions such as finance, marketing, production, etc.

Solution: New management. A chief operating officer may be hired to run operations while existing management steps aside or moves upstairs to a figure-head role. If existing management owns the company, this solution may fail because of unwillingness to relinquish authority. Specialists can be hired to manage such functions as finance and operations. If existing management is adaptable, this may be sufficient change.

Another possibility worth considering either alone or in conjunction with those previously mentioned is strengthening the board of directors. Also, it should be ensured that the board takes an active role in the company's direction, policy making, etc.

Lack of management depth. Frequently, the founder/owner/manager is unwilling to relinquish authority or share management responsibility. Consequently, succession management is not developed. This results in a lack of infusion of new ideas, no one serves as devil's advocate, management is stretched too thin to be effective, no one steps in if management becomes sick, invalid, or absent.

Solution: Addition of back-up management is the most logical and desirable solution. However, the current manager rarely will hire someone of the caliber and independence needed to take charge. More likely, a "gofer" is hired who may be helpful in reducing workload and may solve the management shortfall temporarily. The real problem is encountered, though, when the owner dies or retires and the gofer takes over. The best solution may be life insurance on the owner, and a plan to get out of the credit if management changes.

Management is overleveraged. The company's growth has resulted in a more complex and sophisticated organization. There is a need for experienced and capable managers in key positions. Because of rapid growth, however, the company has not had time to develop the number of skilled managers needed. Either poor decisions are made or control is centralized, and the company cannot respond quickly to problems and opportunities.

Solution: In the early stages, the options include slowing growth while improving the training programs, hiring capable managers from outside the company, or growing through acquisition of well-managed companies. In later stages, when the management shortcomings have an adverse impact on performance, the solution may be drastic reductions in growth, divestiture of subsidiaries, or a crash hiring program.

Weak or incompetent management. Management lacks basic intelligence or skills to run the company.

Solution: Incompetent management must be replaced, or the bank should exit the credit, voluntarily. The only thing worse than incompetence is dishonesty, and neither can be dealt with effectively. Replacing management is a delicate issue. If handled improperly, the bank can potentially become a "control party" and subject to suits from other creditors.

Even if successful, there is often resentment toward the bank and the relationship may be damaged irreconcilably.

Weak management—intelligent but indecisive—can often be bolstered by the addition of new and strong managers. However, the danger is that weak management will hire more weak management. A hiring committee should be formed, consisting of members of the board and possibly outside consultants, to ensure that new management is, in fact, capable.

Management controls and systems are inadequate. Controls mean planning and budgeting, accounting systems, accounts receivable, inventory, payables, and overhead. Although poor controls is a management problem, it is not unusual for an otherwise well-managed company to have partially inadequate systems and controls. In the early stages of a company's growth, adequate controls can often be exercised by "hip pocket" procedures. Later, growth can obscure the need.

Consequently, a company can outgrow its controls without significant adverse repercussions. However, if the situation continues uncorrected, the company's financial health will suffer from uncollectible accounts receivables, unsalable or excess inventory, overspending, high financing costs, poor pricing from lack of good cost data, inadequate management information, and poor planning.

Solution: Fortunately, controls and systems can be improved, if caught in time. This change alone often has dramatic effects on the company's operating efficiency and financial condition. CPAs and consultants can assist in the appraisal of controls and their improvement or replacement. A new financial manager can be hired to install and maintain new systems.

Recession

Many companies find it difficult to operate profitably in a recessionary economy. Consequently, during recessions banks can expect to see many borrowers struggling with reduced sales, higher costs, and other symptoms. By understanding the effects of a recession and the types of companies which are best and worst at coping, it should be easier to anticipate problems and to react more quickly.

Recession-sensitive companies usually experience:
- Declining sales—when housing starts are off carpet companies, furniture companies, and lumber companies suffer.
- Increasing costs associated with inflation—labor, overhead.
- Increasing interest expense.
- Pressure on accounts receivable as customers slow their payments.
- Potential inventory shortages as suppliers become reluctant to stockpile items which are selling slowly.

These signs indicate a potentially severe strain on cash for those companies most susceptible to recession. At the very time that sales are dropping, costs are rising. At the time when cash is most needed, customers are paying more slowly and sellers are demanding faster payment. Some companies cannot cope with these conditions for the duration of a recession and become prime candidates for the problem loan list. Following are some characteristics of companies that can and cannot cope effectively with recession.

Companies which *thrive* are:

• Market leaders and low-cost producers. These are the very well-managed companies which can often gain market share at the expense of their weaker competitors.

• Companies which are countercyclical. The classic example is the liquor store. An increase in the misery index equates to an increase in alcohol consumption—though cheap alcohol. Auto spare parts manufacturers are another example. Car purchases are deferred, and more is spent on upkeep of aging models.

• Growth company in a growth industry. It could be a fad or a new product whose potential has not been reached so sales growth continues despite recession.

• Companies selling products the demand for which is inelastic or luxury items. Even they may suffer if recession is severe enough.

Companies which *stay alive* and reasonably healthy are:

• Companies with strong balance sheets. Liquidity is high, leverage is low. Consequently, the company can live off its own liquidity or borrow.

• Companies in growth industries where momentum offsets the negative impact of the recession.

• Companies with shrewd management that responds quickly to recessionary pressures and protects its downside by cutting fixed costs, reducing debt, etc.

• Companies with a financial structure that allows them to generate significant cash from a sales decline. These companies generally have a low fixed-cost structure and a large investment in accounts receivable or inventory. As sales decline, accounts receivable and inventory are liquidated generating cash. The cash is applied to debt, thus reducing interest expense. Because costs are variable, the company still generates a profit despite reduced sales.

• Companies with products the demand for which is reasonably inelastic or where there is a near monopoly situation.

Companies which *survive*, though barely and only by drastic measures are:

• Companies with a high fixed-cost base that face mounting losses as sales decline but survive by reducing the break-even sales level through:

1. Selling or closing unprofitable lines, subsidiaries, territories, or plants.
2. Reducing salaries and laying off employees.
3. Subcontracting rather than manufacturing component parts.
4. Sale and lease back of assets.
5. Refinancing debt.
6. Increasing prices and reducing sales, hence financing requirements and costs (if interest costs are a major part of the cash flow problem).

• Companies which should have been staying alive, but because management reacted slowly have been financially crippled—companies with strong balance sheets or product demand.

Companies which *take a dive*, that is, companies which fail include:

• Companies that lack sufficient financial or managerial resources.

• Companies operating near cash break-even with a cash flow that becomes negative when sales decline—a company with fixed costs that cannot be cut significantly.

• Companies with few salable assets or other means of reducing break-even.

• Relatively new companies which are still net cash users (borrowers) and have neither financial nor management maturity.

From these examples, we can extract several factors that should be analyzed in framing a company's recessionary profile.

1. *Management.* Is it experienced and capable of dealing with recessionary conditions?

2. *Financial structure.* Is the balance sheet strong enough to withstand a downturn? Does income statement and cost structure allow flexibility on the downside?

3. *Sales sensitivity to recession.* What is the likely impact on sales? Is there countercyclicality or inelasticity?

4. *Financial flexibility.* Does it have an ability to sell assets, cut costs, and take other measures to withstand the financial brunt of recession—generate cash, reduce break-even?

5. *Product demand and position in life cycle.* Is it a new product and a still unexploited market? Is demand so strong that recession will not have much impact?

Some companies' profile indicates that they can virtually ignore a recession. Others can withstand it by taking prudent measure to cut costs and operate lean and efficient. Still others can survive only by drastic measures—selling assets, closing plants, etc. The least fortunate may not make it. The account officer should understand a customer's recessionary profile and be prepared to react at the first signs of recession.

Growth

Growth is usually a healthy and welcome sign of a company's vitality. However, overaggressive or uncontrolled growth can cripple a company. The difficulty is for company management and the bank to recognize when growth has accelerated too rapidly and is approaching the danger zone.

Some warning signs include:

• High financial leverage. Increasing debt with attendant problems of high vulnerability to interest costs and high fixed costs in the form of principal payments.

• Management leverage. Key people spread too thin and key positions filled by inexperienced managers. Especially dangerous with companies growing internally (rather than by merger or acquisition) and in companies which are management intensive, that is, require management for subsidiary companies, stores, departments, etc.

• Company reaching for sales. The result is poorer quality customers and slower accounts receivable turns as marginal customers pay slower or not at all. Larger write-offs of bad debts.

• Inventory turns slow as company loses control over more complex purchasing requirements.

• Overhead grows as former systems become inadequate to control costs in expanded company.

• Returns and allowances increase as production is strained and quality suffers.

• Margins shrink because company accounting systems are insufficient to accurately determine and allocate costs.

• Management becomes reactive. Because of strain on top management to keep day-to-day operations functioning smoothly, management has less time to spend on strategic planning and becomes more oriented toward problem solving.

• Organizational structure becomes anachronistic. As the company grows, several forces emerge, often unnoticed, which must be met by a constant updating in the company's organization structure and dynamics. Functions which could previously be handled as secondary responsibilities now are so large and important that they must be managed independently, for example, personnel and finance. Because of the increasing complexity of the business, there is a greater need for specialization and sophistication in handling the various functions, such as sales and marketing.

Top management must devote more time to strategic planning and general management. Many companies which were founded by entrepreneurs whose background was sales or engineering cannot make the adjustments necessary and the company outgrows them. What had been a healthy, growing company mysteriously begins experiencing problems that may seem temporary to the unexperienced banker, but which are basic and dangerous if not corrected.

The elements of the solution depend on the severity and complexity of the problems. In some cases, merely introducing more sophisticated management controls or creating an awareness in management of the problem is enough. In other cases, management must be completely realigned, possibly with the founder and driving force moved upstairs. This can be a delicate issue and may be possible only if the board of directors sees the need for such drastic action.

Other possible elements of a solution include:

- Bring in a consultant to improve systems and controls.
- Hire a financial officer and other needed specialists.
- Hire an operating officer (general manager).
- Slow growth—possibly even reverse it.
- Sell off portions of the business.
- Replace management.
- Sell the company.

Competition

When a strong competitor moves into the market with a similar or substitute product, the impact on a vulnerable company can be lost sales, reduced margins, increased costs, and loss of key personnel. Unless the entry of a competitor has the beneficial effect of expanding the market and increasing total demand for the product, the vulnerable company can expect a permanent impact and must make permanent adjustments. For example, if sales are reduced, it may be necessary to shrink the company and bring overhead and expenses in line with the new sales level.

In some instances, the well-capitalized company may react offensively by stepping up its marketing effort. Greater emphasis may be placed on brand identification or product differentiation. A change in marketing strategy may be required in order to establish a niche. This could result in higher costs for marketing surveys and promotions and added marketing staff. Alternatively, resources could be reduced as the result of price discounts or a strategy of competitive pricing.

The result of either the defensive or offensive reactions can be long-term financial viability. However, the result of either could be a greatly altered financial structure, that is, higher costs, lower profits, and less sales with implications for the company's growth and debt capacity, dividend payment ability, etc.

Other Causes

Possibly less prevalent, but nonetheless, important cause of problems include:

• Environmental factors. Natural disaster such as drought or flood which can cause a shortage or price increase in raw materials and damage or destroy plant and equipment.

• Regulatory changes. Laws that create expenses without a commensurate increase in productivity, for example, pollution control and minimum wage laws, which can drive costs up and profits down.

• Technological obsolescence. Introduction of advanced technology may render competing products obsolete or at least reduce their value. Improvements in production efficiencies which result from improved technology can provide a competitive advantage.

• Obsolete physical plant. The steel industry is an example of what can happen when obsolete plant and production methods are being used. Imported steel produced in more modern foundries was able to benefit from cost and production efficiencies to gain a competitive advantage. Not only is an obsolete plant a potential cause of a company's problem but it is also a possible obstacle to a successful turnaround. The costs of modernizing, replacing, or expanding may be a prohibitive given the company's limited financial resources.

• Industry change. Too often, permanent changes in an industry are misinterpreted by company management as temporary, that is, the result of a poor economy. For example, a change in the cost or availability of raw materials or saturation or maturity of the market would indicate a need for basic adjustments in the company's operations. However, basic adjustments are not made and conditions deteriorate to the point where options are limited when the real problem becomes evident.

• Sociological trends. Changes in lifestyle and changing trends or fads can completely negate the demand for a product or the method of delivery. For example, as the auto developed as the primary means of transportation and city dwellers flocked to the suburbs, shopping patterns changed from specialty shops such as bakeries and butchers, to large suburban supermarkets.

All these causes have some common elements. They are all external causes which cannot be controlled or corrected by company management. Management can only react by making adjustments to the business. These can be as simple as reorienting the market strategy or more complex such as changing the entire nature of the business. Other possibilities include relocation to follow the customer base, shrinking the company to meet the reduced demand, or possibly closing shop when the sociological change results in a drastic loss of revenues. For a more extensive listing of internal and external factors, see pages 72–74 in Chapter 4, "Analyzing Problem Loans."

Selected Warning Signs

The presentation of a specific list of warning signs has been deferred until the end of the chapter because of the potential for misuse. Reliance on a list of red flags without an understanding of each borrower's unique characteristics and norms can lead to mistaken conclusions and precipitous actions by the banker. However, a list can be valuable as a menu of possible symptoms which must be analyzed in the context of a borrower's specific profile. The following select list includes those signals which in our opinion are the most deserving of further analysis. A more extensive list can be found at the end of this chapter.

Rapid expansion into unrelated field of business. Investment of resources large enough to place a strain on the company.

Rapid sales growth—especially in a management-intensive or skilled-labor-intensive company. Rapid sales growth without a commensurate increase in equity.

Large growth in assets without a commensurate increase in sales.

Deterioration in the return on assets. (Represents company's ability to efficiently utilize assets to generate a profit. More appropriate measure than the return on equity since low equity can result in high returns.)

Significant increase in the debt to equity ratio.

Inventory increasing much more rapidly than sales—inventory turnover slowing.

Large decline in sales or profits.

Large increase in nonproductive assets, especially as a per cent of total assets.

Churning of management—top or middle management.

Difficulty obtaining timely or accurate information—financial or otherwise.

Frequent change in CPAs or frequent change in accounting procedures.

Communications problems between borrower and bank—borrower unresponsive, evasive.

Complex and confusing intercompany transactions which are not clearly explained.

Inordinate increase in accruals—may indicate a need to preserve cash.

Large loans from or borrowings to officers and principals.
Change in personal behavior of principals.
Poor performance against plan.
Radical change in borrowing patterns.
Radical change in financial structure of company—may be moving liabilities off the balance sheet.
Excessive credit checks by suppliers or creditors.
Excessive returns and allowances.
Change in payment terms by suppliers or creditors.
Failure to meet loan agreement covenants.
Past dues, overdrafts, inability to pay out seasonal debt.

Summary

The detection of developing problems cannot be based simply on the existence of good systems. Early detection requires several elements. First, good loan underwriting is needed to ensure that the relationship is established on the basis of a good flow of information between borrower and bank; second, a well-trained account officer who knows the borrower well enough to recognize deviation in performance. Third, good credit administration is needed to back the account officer with systems and support.

When the first signs of a developing problem loan appears, immediate action should be taken to determine the causes. If the cause is within management's conrol, a plan should be developed to solve it. If the cause is beyond management's control, it must be determined if the company can make the necessary adjustments to remain viable despite the problem. Development of a strategy to protect the bank and to deal with the problem starts with information gathering and requires a thorough analysis of the situation.

Early Financial Warning Signals*

Balance Sheet

- Failure to get statements in a timely fashion
- Slowdown in receivables collection period
- Deterioration in customer's cash position
- Sharp increases in dollar amounts or percentage of accounts receivable
- Sharp increase in dollar amounts or percentage of inventory
- Slowdown in inventory turnover
- Decline in current assets as a percentage of total assets
- Deterioration of the liquidity/working capital position
- Marked changes in mix of trading assets
- Rapidly changing concentrations in fixed assets
- Large increase in reserves
- Concentrations in noncurrent assets, other than fixed assets
- High concentration of assets in intangibles
- Disproportionate increases in current debt
- Substantial increases in long-term debt
- Low equity, relative to debt
- Significant changes in balance sheet structure
- Presence of debt due to/due from officer/stockholders

- Unqualified audit
- Change of accounts

Income Statement

- Declining sales
- Rapidly expanding sales
- Major gap between gross and net sales
- Rising cost percentages/narrowing margins
- Rising sales and falling profits
- Rising levels of bad debt losses
- Disproportionate increases in overhead, relative to sales
- Rising levels of total assets, relative to sales/profits
- Operating losses

Receivables Aging

- Extended average age of receivables
- Changes in credit politics
- Extended terms
- Replacement of accounts receivable with notes receivable
- Concentrations of sales
- Compromise of accounts receivable
- Concentrations of seriously past due accounts
- Receivables from affiliated companies

Early Management Warning Signals

- Change in behavior/personal habits of key people
- Marital problems
- Change in attitude toward bank or banker, especially a seeming lack of cooperation

- Failure to perform personal obligations
- Changes in management, ownership, or key personnel
- Illness or death of key personnel
- Inability to meet commitments on schedule

*Jay M. McDonald and John E. McKinley, *Corporate Banking* (Washington, D.C., American Bankers Association, 1981) p. 387–89. Reprinted with permission.

- Recurrence of problems presumed to have been solved
- Inability to plan
- Poor financial reporting and controls
- Fragmented functions
- Venturing into acquisitions, new business, new geographic area, or new product line
- Desire and insistence to take business gambles and undue risk
- Unrealistic pricing of goods and services
- Neglect or discontinuance of profitable standard lines
- Delay in reacting to declining markets or economic conditions
- Lack of visible management succession
- One-man operations showing growth patterns that strain the capacity of the owner to manage and control
- Change in the business, economy, or industry
- Labor problems

Early Operations Warning Signals

- Change in the nature of the company's business
- Poor financial records and operating controls
- Inefficient layout of plant and equipment
- Poor use of people
- Loss of key product lines, franchises, distribution rights, or sources of supply
- Loss of one or more major, financially sound customers
- Substantial jumps in size of single orders
- or contracts that would strain existing productive capacity
- Speculative inventory purchases that are out of line with normal puchasing practices
- Poor maintenance of plant and equipment
- Deferred replacement of outmoded or inefficient plant and equipment
- Evidence of stale inventory, large levels of inventory, or inappropriate mix of inventory

Early Banking Warning Signals

- Declining bank balances
- Excessive note renewals or unanticipated note renewals
- Poor financial planning for fixed asset requirements or working capital requirements
- Heavy reliance on short-term debt
- Marked changes in the timing of seasonal loan requests
- Sharp jumps in the size/frequency of loan requests
- Loans where more than a single source of repayment cannot be easily or realistically identified
- Loans where the purpose is "working capital"
- Calls from existing suppliers requesting credit information to evaluate requests for special terms or expanded credit information to further evaluate the company
- Calls from new supliers, requesting credit information to open new credit lines
- Appearance of other lenders in the financial picture, especially collateral lenders
- Evidence of checks written against uncollected funds

Gathering Information 3

Analysis of a problem is often complicated by lack of reliable information on which to base decisions. Too often the borrower is initially uncooperative because he or she perceives the problem as temporary or not severe and bank interference is resented. In an unfriendly workout, management is reluctant to divulge information that could result in an unwanted plan.

Even in a friendly workout, the information may be poor. If the company's problems stem from, or are exaggerated by, inadequate management controls, then management information will be limited or unreliable. Given time, reasonably good information can be pieced together from various sources. However, the workout officer probably faces time pressures as the situation deteriorates, and he or she must be able to respond quickly. Although the information needed in each situation differs, there is basic information that is useful in most situations and sources which can be tapped to assist in the information-gathering process.

Information Needed

Bank Files

The best source to begin the information gathering and analysis process is the bank's own files—including the credit, documentation, and correspondence files, if they are separate entities. From these sources, a wealth of background information can be mined, if the files have been properly documented. Examples of what might be learned include:

- The relationship between banker and borrower. This may be valuable insight into the account officer's potential effectiveness in handling the workout or the cooperation which can be expected from the borrower in the workout.

- Whether the account officer recognized the developing problem and took effective early measures to deal with it. This may be another indication of the account officer's ability to continue to handle the relationship as workout becomes increasingly more complex.

- Financial statements or correspondence may provide clues to the cause and nature of the problem. In-depth financial analysis has to be performed as part of the process to determine cause and solution. Correspondence may reveal a basic "people" or "communication" problem which may have to be remedied before any other action can be effective. For example, if management refuses to acknowledge the existence of a problem or if there is a personality conflict between banker and borrower, there is little chance for success of a workout plan suggested by the bank.

• Legal vulnerability or advantage. A review of the loan documents may reveal a deficiency which could undermine the bank's collateral position. If collateral has been inadequately described, it may be difficult to prove that a perfected security interest exists or supersedes that of another creditor who has filed with a more specific description. Documents might also be faulty because the effective date has lapsed, because of conflicts in the documents, incomplete documents, or filing in the wrong place. Problems in documentation may suggest that the bank moves cautiously in relations with the borrower until defects can be corrected.

• A bonanza may be discovered by the banker who consciously filed on equipment and failed to realize that in the documents' "boilerplate" there was a dragnet clause which provided for a security interest in the borrower's accounts and deposits.

• Debtor defenses. In a problem loan situation, a debtor often seeks every possible source of leverage available to hold the bank at bay while the company pursues its best interest. The use of debtor defenses has recently become a prominent tool for leverage in the bankruptcy proceeding. For example, if the bank and borrower are at odds over the best plan of action for the company in Chapter 11, the borrower's counsel very probably will subpoena the bank's files. Counsel is looking for evidence of actions which might indicate that the bank has been calling the shots for the company and has become a "control party." If the assertion is valid, the bank could not only lose its loan but also assume responsibility for other borrower liabilities.

• In reviewing the file, any evidence should be examined which would suggest a possible debtor defense. Workout specialists and legal counsel should be involved. They are more adept at recognizing possible defenses and can use the information in formulating the bank's strategy for handling the relationship.

• It is almost always to be expected that the bank's files will be the subject of "discovery" whenever there is litigation in a problem loan situation. It is hoped that files have been documented with this possibility in mind. However, there may be information which is not advantageous to the bank's cause in the file. As a matter of normal procedures, files may be purged in conformity with the bank records retention policies. However, if litigation has already been initiated, even this type of purge should be considered only with the advice of legal counsel.

• It is possibly surprising to the neophyte in workouts that the bank's files can play such an important role. But with the increasing legal complexities associated with problem loan workouts, even the close review of files requires the assistance of specialists and lawyers who are experienced at "sniffing out" possible problems and opportunities. In addition, the account officer's supervisor or credit administration may have to be involved to decide who will handle the workout in the future.

Exposure/Risk

After the bank's own files have been examined, the next priority is to determine from other sources the bank's exposure and the potential for loss. By reviewing public records, the company liabilities and the bank's collateral position, a composite view can be developed of the bank's exposure and its situation relative to other creditors.

Review of Public Records

A check of public records can be useful to verify information provided by management or as a source when that information is unavailable or unreliable. Public records should be checked first to verify that the bank's interests are perfected as intended and to determine if other parties have an interest in the bank's collateral.

Courthouse checks are also a part of the discovery process to determine if there are hidden assets or liabilities or unknown creditors. If the borrower is a closely held company, records of principals and related companies should also be checked.

Records checked and information sought include:

• Real estate records to determine what properties are owned by the borrower and what liens exist on the property and in whose name. In addition, the records should indicate any real estate which has been sold or transferred and any foreclosures by other creditors.

• UCC filing index to determine the security interest filed by other parties in the borrower's personal property and to determine the need to file continuation statements to extend the bank's interest in collateral.

• General execution docket to discover any judgments against the borrower and to locate the judgment documents that will reveal the date and amount of judgments, payments made, or other relevant information. The bank should check the suit dockets to determine any suits pending which have not yet gone to judgment.

• Tax records to determine if there are federal or state tax liens which indicate unpaid taxes. Not only are tax liens a potential drain on cash resources but they could result in the bank's loss of prior secured interest in receivables and inventory if liens are not satisfied within a specified time period.

Company Liabilities

The company's creditors, the amount they are owed and their collateral should be determined. A creditor's absolute exposure and exposure relative to others may prompt them to actions which are reasonably predictable and which should be anticipated by the banker. For example, a major supplier may cut off the company's vital product supply. A large and well-secured creditor may use the threat of foreclosure as leverage to be "bought out" of the credit by other creditors. Large unsecured creditors may pose the threat of bankruptcy which could be detrimental to the bank's interests.

Analysts should not only examine listed liabilities but should also investigate the company's "hidden liabilities." Hidden liabilities are those that either do not appear on the financial statement or that appear but cannot be easily understood or determined. They represent real obligations of the borrower and could greatly affect a workout. Examples include:

- Pension liabilities.
- Lease obligations—especially in the case of a building owned by a principal of the company and leased to the company.
- Intercompany debt—intercompany accounts receivable may represent noncollectible assets.
- Parent company obligations—the parent may require upstreaming of funds as management fees, consulting fees, dividends, loans, etc.
- Subsidiary company obligations—a subsidiary may be fed to keep it funded, especially if it is losing cash or is a net cash user.
- Contingent liabilities—lawsuits, guarantees.
- Merchandise or service-provided disputes—especially problematical with a company in bankruptcy. As an example, contractor receivables are often difficult to collect. Service warranties may have to be satisfied.
- Principal's debt—especially in closely held companies where principal and company cannot be separated. The obligation of one is essentially an obligation of the other.

Collateral

The bank's true exposure depends on the ability to realize on its collateral if the company fails. Previously, the bank files and the courthouse records should have verified the legal claims to collateral and identified possible clouds on title from improper documentation or conflicting claims of other creditors. Next, the collateral must be located and valued. Deterioration of collateral values is commonplace in problem situations where the company has sold the best inventory, collected the best accounts receivable, and failed to properly maintain and service plant and equipment.

Values in liquidation must consider the condition and salability of collateral and its value in liquidation as opposed to book or going concern value. There will be liquidation costs and carrying costs if collateral must be liquidated but is not readily salable. If the company's problem is its inability to sell its product, the likelihood is great that the bank's collateral may be the same assets which the company cannot sell. The ability to determine the bank's net collateral protection or exposure may be a major factor in its willingness to continue to work with the borrower.

The comparison of going concern versus liquidation value may dictate a particular workout strategy or liquidation strategy. For example, if collateral is easily salable in its present state, an immediate liquidation may be feasible. If it must be processed for sale, the necessity to continue operations becomes apparent. Collateral is covered in greater detail in Chapter 7.

Agings and Concentrations

Agings and concentrations are listed because of the possible implications for the valuation of collateral. They could also be considered part of the financial category because of cash flow and general asset quality.

• Accounts receivable aging is a breakout by age categories such as 30, 60, 90 days and older (listed in dollar and percent aggregates). For example, an aging might indicate that $100,000 or 6% of total accounts receivables are over 60 days old. It is helpful to track trends in agings and to assess deterioration in accounts receivable quality. This is especially important information if accounts receivable are pledged as collateral. The aging also provides a good indication of the collectibility of the receivables—one of the primary sources of a company's cash inflow.

• Inventory agings are not always available because of loss of identity by comingling in bulk storage or in the manufacturing process. However, agings can be useful in situations where inventory consists of large ticket items such as farm or construction equipment. Old inventory may indicate poor purchasing practices or possible loss of demand. It may also mean the loss of value of collateral or have negative implications for cash flow. When inventory is collateral and there is concern for its value or existence, a physical inventory may be advisable. This can be conducted by an independent agency such as a certified public accountant, by the bank, or by the company in a supervised situation.

• Accounts payable agings. If payables are becoming seriously past due, the potential exists for legal action and for loss of supplier sources.

The ability to establish a workout plan may depend on reasonable satisfaction of supplier credit. Also, suppliers may have to be drawn into the workout plan to assure continued ability to obtain product. If supplier indebtedness is large and long past due, there may be insufficient funds to both satisfy creditors and provide financing for the company's rehabilitation. Consequently, the status of payables may be a major consideration in the determination of workout strategy.

• Accounts receivable concentrations, a detailed listing of accounts receivables, indicate concentrations from the largest customers. With a concentration of accounts in a delinquent status, an investigation will be necessary to determine the ability to pay and general creditworthiness of the individual customers.

• Accounts payable concentrations are important because large suppliers may push the company into bankruptcy or cut off raw materials supply. When payables are concentrated in several suppliers, vulnerability increases, and the bank may face the reality that their prior secured interest in inventory is valuable only in an immediate liquidation. In a workout, the suppliers have great negotiating leverage, and they may refuse to sell without security.

Financial/Management Information

It is impossible to structure a workout plan without an understanding of the company's basic financial viability and the cash resources needed to effect the turnaround. Financial management is also an important ingredient in the company's ability to solve its problems and to manage scarce cash resources in the process.

Statements and Projections

The need for statements and projections is so basic that they should have been obtained as part of the loan decision and administration process. If past statements are not on file, they should be obtained and analyzed to determine when the symptoms of a problem first appeared and the extent of the financial impact. In-depth analysis of statements is necessary to determine the company's basic viability and to derive the assumptions which can be reasonably proposed for projections of future viability. If actual and projected performance have varied widely, statements should be analyzed again and projections recast.

If available, detailed breakouts of the statements are helpful in analyzing results by product group, by subsidiary, or by sales territory. Detailed information on expenses can identify those which are fixed and variable and those which are prospects for the chopping block.

Good quality statement information is crucial in the assessment of problem causes and in devising solutions. It may also be necessary to increase the frequency of preparation of financial statements to a weekly or monthly basis. In a financial crisis, frequent statements are needed to monitor progress or deterioration, to measure the impact of changes, and to better manage and control. If the quality of information is poor, upgrading the preparers may be necessary. Since reliable information depends on internal control systems, it may be necessary to employ certified public accountants (CPAs) or consultants who can assist in establishing good controls as well as the preparation of reports.

Cash Budget

In a workout, the ability to preserve and generate cash is the key to the company's survival in the short term. The cash budget details the sources and uses of cash and the resulting excess or shortage for each period. It identifies those sources which are steady and dependable and those uses which chew up the largest amounts of cash. It also identifies those uses which are candidates for deferral or reduction. It provides the banker with the best tool for deriving additional borrowing needs and determining the company's ability to become cash viable within a reasonable period—before additional borrowing needs become so great that the company is swamped by a flood of debt.

Capital Budget

This schedule of proposed capital expenditures helps identify prospects for cut backs, deferrals, or elimination, thereby reducing cash outflow.

Strategic Plan

Not all companies have a written plan. However, even companies without a stated plan should have a strategic concept of where management wants the company to go and how it should get there. This concept should be supported by detailed plans for action. However, lack of planning is often the root of problems. Management, for example, may have become so absorbed in the day-to-day aspects of the business that it has forgotten to plan for the future. Or management may have planned but poorly, and the present strategy has failed in the marketplace or within the company.

If a written plan is available, it should be scrutinized not only to determine its reasonableness but also how well it is being executed. If no plan is available, management should be interviewed to determine the nature of its plan and how it is being implemented. If the company stock is publicly traded, it must prepare and make available a 10K report. This provides information on products, plans, and markets which can reveal a company's basic strategic thrust.

Analysis of a company's strategic plan may identify problems which are reversible in the short or intermediate term, for example, improving plan implementation. It may also reveal more far-reaching problems which can be solved only by a basic change in strategy.

CPA Management Letter

If a CPA firm audits company operations, the company receives a management letter with the audit. It outlines any systems and controls problems and other recommendations that arise as a result of the auditing process. This can be obtained from the company and can provide insight into possible management or systems problems.

Tax Return

If financial statements are company-prepared or of seemingly poor quality, it may be prudent to obtain the company's tax return. Although the information cannot be directly compared with a statement based on accrual accounting, it can provide invaluable insight into the company's financial performance and condition.

When the business is a closely held company or the debt is personally guaranteed, the principal's or guarantor's tax return might also be obtained since the income/expenses/obligations of the individuals and the company are in many ways inseparable.

Corporate Checking Account

Monitoring the checking account can provide valuable insight into how the company allocates its cash. It may indicate a change in suppliers as old suppliers switch to cash only terms, or it may indicate movements of funds out of the business. Large payments to other creditors that are applying considerable "heat" may be noticed.

The personal checking account of the principal of the closely held company should also be watched. Comingling of funds and assets between owner and company is fairly easy. Also, the personal spending habits of the principal indicate a change in personal behavior that was listed as a warning signal in the previous chapter.

External Environment

In isolating causes of problem loans, the banker has to consider the impact of such external factors as governmental regulation, sociological change, the industry, and competition. Although there are many possibilities in any given situation, there are several factors which should always be considered.

Industry/Competitor Information

The company's performance should be measured against competitors and peers in the industry to determine if all are suffering equally. If so, the industry must be more closely analyzed to determine its basic characteristics and expectations for turnaround. For example, if the industry has matured, growth will have stagnated, competition will be severe, and the strongest and best managed survive without major realignments. Weaker companies, however, may have to take drastic action to ensure survival.

If the company's problems are unique, it still may be because of its relative position within its industry. If the company is a marginal producer in a cyclical industry, it will realize strong profits only at the top of the business cycle. At the bottom of the cycle, sales fall drastically and profitability disappears. Another cause of the company's problems might be its failure to have established a market niche, despite the fact that it is too small to compete with the largest and financially strongest companies in the industry.

Information on the industry may be available from the bank's own files, by contacting other companies in the industry, through trade reports or magazines, from trade associations, stock brokers or investment houses, from other bankers, and from suppliers or customers. The sources are numerous, and the effective workout officer has to be resourceful in gathering this and other forms of information.

Trade and Other Creditors and Customers

The decision to check with other creditors is not automatic. In the early stages of a problem, the experience of creditors can be beneficial. However, if the problem is advanced, any call on other creditors may serve as a red flag that alerts them to the problem or its severity. It may even prompt them to actions which would be detrimental to the bank. If the decision is made to contact other creditors, the call should be handled by an experienced banker who can reach the most appropriate party, ask the right questions, and recognize unresponsive or evasive respondents.

Customers may also be sources of valuable insight on the company. If quality or service has suffered, it may indicate financial or operational problems that could result in sales reductions and additional financial difficulties.

Obtaining Information

The account officer should be the best source of information and should ensure a constant stream of valuable information through the loan underwriting and administration process. This information is useful in problem loan detection and analysis. However, when less conventional means of obtaining information are necessary, many account officers cannot respond. Most account officers lack the training or technical skill to intelligently examine a company's internal financial records and must seek expert assistance. Possible sources of assistance include:

• The bank's workout specialists and experienced credit people. Bankers who have been through the workout process before and have dealt with recalcitrant borrowers not only can provide guidance and counsel but can also serve as the bank's negotiating agent. Often an unknown third party of some perceived authority can more successfully gain a borrower's cooperation.

• The bank's internal auditors. These people can provide insight into the condition of financial systems such as purchasing, paying, accounts receivable approval and collection, and expense controls. Also, they can usually report on the status of receivables and payables and possibly inventory, depending on the condition of financial records.

• CPAs. They provide the same service as the bank's auditors and also provide an audit of the company's specific assets, for example, inventory and receivables. They can determine the adequacy of systems and controls *and* can provide recommendations to improve existing systems or assist the company in the installation of better systems and controls. CPAs can establish management reports and reporting procedures to ensure the flow of reliable information in the future.

• Consultants. This group can either augment the efforts of the previously mentioned parties, can do the same things, and more. They can delve into the problem and its causes and offer a management perspective in determining possible solutions. They can assess management's capabilities or shortcomings, organizational inefficiencies, corporate objectives, and plans and projections. They can construct financial projections and cash flows and assist in immediate workout and long-range viability planning.

Often the borrower welcomes an independent party's observations and assistance. In some workout situations, the relationship between banker and borrower deteriorates and becomes strained. The introduction of an unbiased third party may be the best means of breaking a deadlocked situation and arriving at an agreement on the company's best alternatives for rehabilitation.

The bank should welcome the use of a consultant since it reduces the likelihood of a lawsuit from other creditors. If the bank suggests, or especially if it dictates, actions to the borrower which later are perceived as detrimental to other creditors, the potential for lawsuit exists. Because of this potential, it is preferable that the consultant be hired by the company to avoid the argument that the consultant acted as agent for the bank.

However, the bank can suggest a list of firms from which the borrower chooses.

Summary

The gathering of information is directed not only toward an analysis of the problem but also toward a "situational analysis". This entails a judgment of the bank's and other creditors' situation, the borrower's situation, and a preliminary evaluation of options. Despite conclusions about the nature and solvability of the problem, the bank's options may be dictated or influenced by such factors as its collateral position or the leverage of other parties. For example, turnaround may appear feasible and in the bank's best interest. However, the threat of bankruptcy proceedings from other creditors may pose an unacceptable risk in a turnaround strategy.

Information gathering should proceed immediately with recognition of problem loan symptoms. Decisions may have to be made and actions taken despite incomplete or unreliable information. However, these actions should be limited to emergency measures designed to buy time. They should not include the establishment of long-range turnaround strategy. Sufficient and reliable information may have been gathered to determine causes and design solutions. However, if turnaround prospects are good, systems and controls must be installed to provide the type of information needed to manage the company and to monitor the progress of the turnaround plan.

Analyzing Problem Loans 4

As the workout process continues, we advance now to the analysis phase. If the cause of the problem is obvious or easy to discern, analysis can be relatively simple. It can also be a long and complex drill that requires a large investment in time and resources to complete.

Before the bank can intelligently select an optimal plan of action, several issues must be resolved. First, the problem symptoms and causes must be identified. A dangerous tendency is to perform only a superficial analysis concluding that symptoms are causes and failing to comprehend the real problem.

Solvability

After causes have been determined, a judgment must be made about the solvability of the problem. The major components of a successful turnaround include:

- Competent management.
- A viable core business.
- Resources sufficient to effect the turnaround.
- A sound strategy based on analysis conclusions.

If the core business is viable, management must be appraised to determine its ability to set the strategies, make the changes, and manage scarce resources to turn the company around. In a workout, management is often faced with shortages of raw materials, money, time, and people. Consequently, the assessment of management must consider that greater skills are required in workout than are needed in general day-to-day management.

Before proceeding, the bank must be satisfied that workout is not only possible but also is in its own best interest. If there is a conviction that turnaround is possible, an estimate must be made of what is needed to get the company from where it is today to where it needs to be. For example, additional management and financial resources may be required and additional risks assumed by both the company and the bank. The potential exists that management's favored plan will involve more risks for the bank than is acceptable. If a compromise cannot be found, the stalemate may have to be broken by resorting to other options such as bankruptcy.

The analysis phase of the workout process can be visualized in the following schematic:

Analysis Schematic

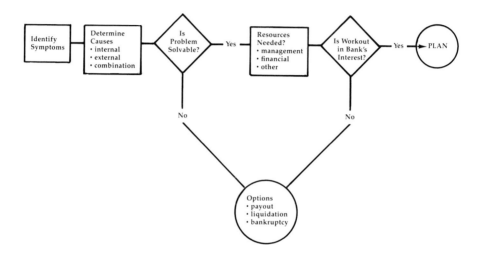

Because problem loan symptoms can be misleading and because there are so many possible sources of problems, it is difficult to design a standard approach to analysis. Workout requires a thorough knowledge of all phases of the business to ensure that causes are correctly analyzed and solutions effective. This chapter does not presume to cover all aspects of analysis but selectively discusses the managerial and financial aspects of analysis which are essential to the workout process.

Management Analysis

Earlier in the book, we identified management as a major cause of company problems or failure. Even when the major cause is not management, it is often management's inability to react and to make the necessary adjustments that ensures the company's failure. Consequently, an analysis of management is necessary even though the cause of problems may have been correctly identified as external to the company, for example, competition or recession.

Management should have been analyzed thoroughly at loan inception and at least annually as part of the loan administration and review procedures. The existence of a potential workout situation, however, suggests the need for more in-depth analysis to determine three main questions:

1. Were previous assessments inadequate or incorrect or have conditions changed sufficiently to effect management's long-term capacity to manage the company? Banks spend considerable time and money training account officers in financial analysis. However, training in management analysis, which is possibly the most important ingredient in a company's success, is usually left to experience. Consequently, the analysis is frequently cursory and based more on gut feel than on a realistic appraisal.

As mentioned, the growth and evolution of a company place different and greater demands on management. Individuals who were competent to run small, easily controlled operations may fail to adapt to changing organizational needs. They may even lack the capacity, skills, and propensity to meet the demands of the larger, more complex corporation.

2. Has existing management the capacity for crisis management? Management, which has been seasoned and proven capable over several years of successful operations, may be unable to cope with a crisis situation. The managers may be emotionally unable to change the way things are done or even to admit that a problem exists. Also, the added stress associated with crisis management may be more than can be handled.

3. Has management the honesty and integrity to warrant the banker's trust? If management's integrity is questionable, there are only two courses of action: change management or exit the relationship. The latter alternative can be to call the loan and liquidate or obtain a take out from another financing source.

Analyzing management in the workout scenario entails many of the same objectives as the initial loan appraisal. This includes a determination of how well management understands its business and the major challenges it faces. Such methods of analyzing management as plant visits and creditor, supplier, and competitor checks are valuable and should be considered. However, the best method of analyzing management is by direct interview with as many key managers of the company as possible. Before the visit, a list of topics and questions should be prepared. This list is to gain insight into the way in which the company is organized and managed, the effectiveness of controls, the ability to generate management information, the abilities of the management team, etc. In addition, the banker should determine if the management team agrees on the company's problems and the best methods of approaching them. In a well-managed company, there should be general agreement about management priorities and objectives and the means of accomplishing them.

General Management Capacity

The following is an example of the types of questions which would indicate how well management understands its business and how well the company is organized and managed. There are five general categories to be examined: organization/personnel, planning/policy, information/systems, marketing, and finance. Others could be added, such as production and sales, depending on the nature of the company and the objectives of the interviewer.

1. Organization/Personnel. How well defined is the company's organizational structure? Is there a clear chain of command? Are job responsibilities clearly defined? Is the organization centralized or decentralized? Are there profit centers or cost centers? What are their specific responsibilities?

Who are the key managers? What are their backgrounds and experience? Are they technicians, generalists? Is their experience in sales, finance, production, engineering, etc.? At what level are major decisions made? Is there a succession of management plan? Are goals and objectives set for managers' performance? How is performance measured and rewarded?

2. Planning/Policy. What is the forum for policy setting and for major decisions? Is it formalized? Which managers participate? Describe the planning process. What's included—strategic planning, financial planning? How often are plans reviewed, altered, updated? How has company performed against plan?

Can the company define the business it is and is not in and outline its goals and objectives, both immediate and long term? Is there a plan for meeting them? How does management define company's strengths and weaknesses? What are major challenges and uncertainties which the company must anticipate and plan for?

What is the make-up of the board of directors? Are there prominent outsiders? What is their role/responsibility? Who are inside members? Who controls the major ownership position(s) in the company? What is the quality of advisors and advice received from professionals retained by company—lawyers, CPAs, or consultants? Is a full audit performed or is the company doing the least it possibly can to save the expense? Are lawyers and advisors of the best quality?

3. Information/Systems. Can management define the key items which must be controlled? Are there systems in place and is reliable management information produced to monitor these items? Are management reports of reasonable quality, thoroughness, scope, and frequency?

Is there exception reporting and management review? For example, are large past-due accounts over 60–90 days old reported so that they receive proper monitoring? Are expenditures over a certain size approved by higher management?

4. Marketing. What is the company's marketing strategy? Is there a detailed plan to support it which includes advertising, pricing, and distribution? How often is a market and competitive assessment made? What is the company's niche or competitive advantage? Is it price, quality, service? What is the customer profile? How does the company determine customer preferences and satisfaction?

5. Finance. Does the company have financial standards and goals for such things as financial leverage, profitability, cash flow, and growth? Are monthly cash and credit needs understood and projected with accuracy? Is the break-even sales level known? Are contribution margins for various products calculated and monitored? Can the company generate reliable cost data?

Crisis Management Capacity

Management's past experience in dealing with a crisis could be a good indicator of its crisis management capacity. However, management may not have had this experience or it may not be known. Consequently, the best measure is a combination of general management capability as covered in the previous section plus management's reaction to the current problem situation.

First, determine management's assessment of the situation. Is it realistic, overly optimistic, or too pessimistic? Overly optimistic management may be slow to act; overly pessimistic management may be losing hope or feeling helpless in the face of the crisis.

Next, analyze management's reaction to the problem. Has a plan been developed? Is it specific with objectives, responsibilities assigned, timetables established, and costs estimated. Have the long-range implications of the problem and needed changes been considered? Who was involved in establishing the plan? Was outside or professional advice sought? How committed is the management team to this plan of action? If there is a detailed plan, it should be a positive indication of management's recognition of the problem and willingness to deal with it.

A manager who is overstressed may be reluctant to admit the existence or severity of the problem. If management has a plan it will be vague and lack specifics. Generally, this type of manager is reluctant to discuss the problem, down plays it, and emphasizes that the company can handle it without interference from the bank. This attitude should be a cause for concern.

When management seems unrealistic about its problems, there should be further analysis to determine the reasons. There are two possibilities to consider:

1. Stress. An overstressed manager will not always act or react rationally and his or her personal behavior will usually reflect the level of stress. If the manager becomes difficult to deal with, irrational, easily irritated, if members of the management team become disgruntled and leave, if top management isolates itself from criticism or advice, stress could be the cause. Additional signs could be health problems, increased drinking habits, or problems at home. Be especially alert to a situation where stress from sources external to the company are added to the internal stresses associated with crisis managerial responsibility.

2. Emotional investment. This stems from several sources. If the problem resulted from top management error or failure, an acknowledgment or admission could result in loss of stature, loss of respect among subordinates, or reduced responsibility. If management feels that clear evidence of a problem will result in dismissal or reduction in responsibility, managers will want to protect their investment by denying the problem.

An emotional investment may arise if management strategy has misfired and the obvious solution is a change in strategy. If management's emotional ties to the strategy are strong, there is a tendency to rationalize problems as temporary setbacks and a reluctance to make the sweeping changes necessary. An example would be the introduction of a new product which fails. Rather than scrap the product and move on, there is a conviction that given time and enough advertising support, it will eventually succeed.

Management's commitment to the strategy or product may eventually ensure its success. However, the danger is that management will be blinded by its emotional commitment and not make rational, objective decisions.

Management Integrity

If the bank concludes that management is less than forthright, it is time for drastic measures. Reasonable decisions cannot be based on unreliable information, and the execution of the plan cannot be carried out by a management team which cannot be trusted.

The incidence of outright fraud or deceit are rare, though certainly not unknown. More often, the bond of trust is broken because management of the troubled company perceives that the bank does not really understand its problems. Therefore, the bank cannot be expected to agree to a reasonable turnaround plan. Communications deteriorate as the company pursues what it believes to be its best option, while attempting to hold the bank at bay. Information provided may not be dishonest but slow in coming or incomplete.

If this situation is allowed to persist and the problem worsens, the bank's collateral and the company's resources may be dissipated. Also, management has committed everything to its own plan and when failure appears evident, there is the realization that under the circumstances the company cannot look to the bank for assistance. Consequently, maximizing personal interests becomes managers' first priority. At this point, the potential for outright fraud and dishonesty greatly increases. What started as a well-intentioned plan by management has degenerated into a divisive struggle in which both parties lose.

The obvious lesson is that the banker must be alert to the signals of an uncooperative management seeking to follow its own course with minimum banker interference. These signals include:

- Late receipt of information.
- Unresponsive to ideas or suggestions.
- Closing and moving checking accounts.
- Evasive answers to direct questions—"we're changing systems and won't have that information for several weeks."
- Attempts to divert the bank's attention to other issues, such as possibility of losing the company's business if "treatment" from the banker doesn't improve.
- Change of CPAs with resulting late statements and changes in accounting procedures.
- Moving liabilities off the balance sheet to subsidiary companies.
- Constantly "unavailable" management.

Turnaround Management

Management is not only the major cause of company failure but it is also the essential element in a successful rehabilitation. Bankers are sometimes surprised when previously successful managers cannot respond to adverse circumstances; but good times can often compensate for bad management. Managing a turnaround situation is much more demanding, and in some cases the problem can only be solved by introducing new management.

The characteristics associated with effective management in a crisis are generally agreed on. In addition to the mental toughness and basic leadership skills required, the individual must also be realistic and fair-minded, open to advice and criticism but willing to stand behind decisions. He or she must have the ability to think strategically, to set plans and objectives, and to marshal the company's resources to get results. The manager should be cool in a crisis and a tough negotiator. Management that has previously experienced adversity and dealt with it successfully is less likely to panic and understands how to function under conditions of scarce resources.

It is not likely that all the desired characteristics will be found in any single manager. But it should be realized that crisis management requires greater skills and analysis than management under normal day-to-day circumstances. Although a cooperative borrower is preferable, it is far better to deal with a tough borrower who has independent ideas and opinions than to have weak managers running the company.

Financial Analysis

Management has been analyzed to determine its part in creating or adding to the company's problems and to determine its ability to solve the problems. Next, analysis shifts to the company's financial peformance to expose causes and to determine the solvability of problems and the viability of the core business.

Basic viability depends on the existence of demand for the product, the ability to generate sufficient sales to exceed break-even, and the ability to consistently produce a positive cash flow from operations. It is not easy to determine viability when the company is losing money and liabilities are mounting rapidly. The inclination is to concentrate on how the company can cope with the losses and spiraling obligations.

Although the company's present condition is a major concern, it must be put aside while efforts are directed toward an analysis of the core business. To restore viability, the company may have to be stripped back to the core, eliminating weak performers and building on strengths. Consequently, weak areas have to be defined and the analysis based on assumptions that changes can be made to restructure the company.

To proceed, assume that the company could start anew without the existing debt and without the weak performers. Will these assumptions enable the company to produce a positive cash flow at reasonable sales levels? If not, the obvious conclusion is that the company can no longer function as a viable entity given its new environment. This might be the case if competition has forced sales or margins so low that the company cannot support its existing cost structure. The painful conclusion is that the company must be sold or liquidated or change its business.

If the company appears viable, there is yet another hurdle before the banker should proceed to workout. That is the added cost and risk involved in restoring viability. To take the company from its present state back to financial stability involves time, money, and people. If the process is too risky and the outcome too uncertain, the added risk cannot be justified. The decision to join with the company in the workout process must be based on a thorough appraisal of the added exposure to the bank and the potential costs, both direct and indirect.

When the company appears viable and the problems solvable, the process moves to establishing a workout plan. However, there must be a bridge to get the company from its present situation to financial solvency. This bridge consists of the financial and other resources needed to keep the company going, while plans and strategies are set and implemented. It is, in effect, an emergency plan.

Analyzing Past Performance

Analysis begins with a search for causes using the financial statements of past periods—years, quarters, months. Rarely is financial analysis an end in itself; it enables the analyst to focus on the relevant issues and to ask the right questions.

Trend and comparison analysis

In a previously profitable and financially healthy company, trend analysis is helpful in isolating deviations that might represent the signs of a problem. Trend analysis alone may indicate a problem but not provide sufficient evidence to determine the cause. For example, if sales were steadily declining a possible conclusion might be marketing ineffectiveness. Comparison with industry data, however, might indicate that the sales decline is industrywide. Therefore, the loss of demand would have to be examined further and the performance of the company compared with the industry to determine management's effectiveness.

Another useful form of comparison is company plans. Performance against plan should be compared for several years to determine the credibility factor. If significant deviation appeared for the first time, it should be easier to focus on the problem. Plans which are historically accurate and regularly updated generally indicate that management is aware of the factors which have an impact on its ability to meet the plan.

Comparison analysis should utilize not only income statements and balance sheets but also funds flow statements and ratios. Sometimes referred to as "where got, where gone" statements, funds flow statements are an excellent source of information on how the company has allocated its resources. For example, it would expose an overinvestment in fixed assets, improper financial structuring, or investments in nonproductive assets. Used in conjunction with ratios, trends can be placed in two perspectives—magnitude of dollar changes and changes in proportion—actual dollar investments in fixed assets and fixed asset investment in relation to sales or total assets.

The profitability trap

The banker should be very cautious not to equate profitability with financial health. A profitable company can experience severe cash shortages as the result of actions which will not affect the income statement immediately. For example:

- The company is outgrowing its equity base. Increasing sales are causing accounts receivable and inventory levels to increase faster than the company's ability to fund them internally.
- Overinvestment in inventory. This appears on the balance sheet but not in the income statement.
- Uncollectible or slowly collectible accounts receivables. Revenues are recorded at the time of sale despite uncollectibility. Profits are overstated.
- Investment in nonproductive assets—land speculation.
- Overinvestment in plant, property, and equipment.

All the above has an impact on the company's cash position without having an immediate impact on profitability. If proper accounting procedures are followed, and that is not always a safe assumption, the inventory and accounts receivable will be written down and the fixed assets depreciated. Consequently, the impact will eventually be reflected on the income statement. However, the analyst must look to the company's cash condition to determine its financial health and basically disregard profits in the short-run when analyzing the problem company.

The most reliable tool for determining the company's cash sources and needs is the cash budget. Management should already be producing a cash budget to determine its weekly cash needs. If not, there probably is limited financial discipline in the company. In a workout, the cash budget is essential, not only for financial discipline but also to allow accurate projections of borrowing needs and to examine the components for undependable sources. It also forces management to carefully consider expenditures and their timing and magnitude.

When the company was healthy, management could depend on its line of credit as a back-up for cash needs. Consequently, detailed cash management was not so crucial. In a cash crisis situation, the banker should be closely supervising any additional advances to the company. Without the cash budget, the ability to anticipiate needs is limited and decisions are often made hastily and under pressure from other creditors.

Strengths and weaknesses analysis

As the statements are reviewed, a worthwhile exercise is to isolate the company's strengths and weaknesses. Financial problems may not arise from major causes such as recession but simply from a combination of subtle weaknesses that when viewed together indicate a generally weak company. In addition, strengths and weaknesses analysis is useful in determining the company's ability to deal with the existing problem and future uncertainties. It may suggest areas which must be strengthened or eliminated when designing a plan for the company's long-range viability.

Key control factors

In virtually every company, there are factors the control of which is crucial to the company's financial performance. For example, it could be portion control in a restaurant, accounts receivable control in a wholesaler, or inventory controls in a manufacturer. During the analysis of a company with financial problems, the key control factors should be identified and the effectiveness of the company's controls determined. Professional assistance, from CPAs or consultants, may be required in situations where drastic action is necessary.

However, in many instances, basic questions are sufficient to ascertain the existence of controls. Some of the most common areas of control include accounts receivable, inventory/purchasing, growth, planning/budgeting, capital expenditures, expenses/overhead, and cash.

Using accounts receivable and inventory as examples of critical areas of control, the following questions help in the evaluation process:

1. Accounts Receivable
- How are credit checks performed on customers and potential customers? What sources are used? How often?
- Are credit limits and terms established for individual customers? Who sets them? What guidelines are followed?
- Who has final approval on a sale—the salesman, manager, or credit person?
- Can the company readily produce an accounts receivable aging? What percentage of receivables is past due? What past-due percentages are considered acceptable? What procedures are followed in collecting past dues? Who reviews them? Who collects them? When are they turned over to a collection agency?
- What is the company's charge-off policy? What has the loss experience been? Is the reserve adequate? How is it determined?

2. Inventory/Purchasing
- What are the company's purchasing procedures? How are purchase orders originated and approved? Who has final authority on what and how much is ordered or reordered?
- On what basis are suppliers selected? How are they screened for quality and dependability? Are there major suppliers which provide more than 15%-20% of the company's product? What is known about their financial condition, management, etc.?
- Is the company using perpetual or periodic inventory methods? Is

inventory computerized with automatic reorder levels pro-
grammed? How are monthly inventory levels/values derived?

- Who is responsible for ensuring that inventory levels are adequate but not excess? What information/reports are used to make this judgment?
- How often are physical inventory counts taken?
- How are manufacturing costs (if appropriate) allocated to inventory?
- How often and on what basis are inventory write-downs made? What has past experience been?

The experienced account officer can readily develop a similar list of questions to determine the existence and effectiveness of controls over such things as expenses, capital expenditures, and cash. Some of the is-sues associated with growth and with planning and budgeting have al-ready been covered in previous chapters.

The banker who is new to workout is often surprised by the impact on a company of basic, seemingly insignificant, changes. The relatively simple steps of improving controls over key factors and more clearly defin-ing responsibility within the organization, for example, are sometimes all that is needed to get a company back on course. In the analysis of causes, "small things" should not be overlooked in anticipation that the cause must be of such magnitude that it will be plainly obvious.

A word of caution is advised. Controls may only be a portion of the problem or the symptoms of a larger (management) problem. If so, im-proving controls may provide only a temporary or partial solution. Un-wary bankers who become overly optimistic at the sign of improvement may later find that because of the failure to identify the real problem, the inevitable has only been delayed.

Projecting Future Performance

This is the most difficult part of the workout process because so much depends on the assumptions which must be made. The less confidence that is felt in the assumptions, the greater the margin for error needed. Our analysis so far has provided the background against which assump-tions about future performance must be judged. Projections include pro forma income statement and balance sheets, cash budgets, sensitivity anal-ysis, break-even and operating leverage analysis, and working investment analysis.

Pro forma analysis

Pro formas have to be cast to determine the possible structure of the balance sheet given the most reasonable and worst case assumptions. If reasonable assumptions cannot be made which indicate a financial structure that can be supported from operations, the options become restructuring or liquidation.

In some instances, the company has outgrown its equity base and is drowning in debt. Conceivably, operations can be scaled back so that a smaller investment in assets is required, and debt can be reduced to manageable levels. This might be accomplished in conjunction with other options, such as additional equity injections or reductions in liabilities from creditors willing to accept a partial payment in full settlement. This is sometimes possible with unsecured creditors that fear a complete loss in bankruptcy.

If the company cannot amortize its regular debt payments, a debt restructuring might be an alternative. If the company's receivables and inventory have value as collateral, an asset-based lender may be able to convert term debt to permanent-type finance and relieve considerable cash strain. This allows the company to grow and thereby increase profits and equity.

Ratio analysis

The analysis of trends using ratios suggested in past analysis should be continued with particular attention to significant projected changes. Also, there are four relationships derived from the income statement and balance sheet which must be in sync to assure long-term financial stability.

1. Sales/Expense Relationship—indicator of the margins necessary to ensure profitability and debt repayment capacity. It is sensitive to a reduction in sales without commensurate expense reductions, as in a company with high fixed costs. In a company with high fixed costs, the probability of sales decreasing as the result of recession or competition should be ascertained and needed margins for error built into the model.

This relationship is also sensitive to expense increases in conjunction with stagnant or declining sales. If the market appears stagnant, the probability of increased expenses from such factors as labor unions or inflation should be analyzed.

2. Profit/Debt Relationship—indicator of the ability to amortize debt. It is sensitive to an increase in debt without a corresponding increase in profit. If this relationship is marginal, the analyst must be concerned with the possibility of additional debt, for example, for plant improvement or to meet environmental regulations.

This relationship is also sensitive to a decline in profitability without the ability to reduce debt. For example, a sales decrease in a capital intensive company may have an impact on profits, but debt will not decrease significantly.

3. Debt/Equity Relationship—indicator of the margins available in the

asset values listed in the balance sheet. Also, it is an indication of a company's "staying power" when facing adversity. The lower the debt in relation to equity, the greater the company's capacity to borrow or to shrink the balance sheet and live off the proceeds.

This relationship is sensitive to rapid growth which increases the investment in assets much faster than the increase in equity. It is also sensitive to decreases in equity as the result of unprofitable operations, treasury stock purchases, etc.

4. Sales/Assets Relationship—indicator of the base level of assets needed to support a certain level of sales. The ratio is sensitive to an overinvestment in assets, rapid growth or decline in sales, and slowly turning assets, such as accounts receivable and inventory. If sales are disproportionately high in relation to assets, it may indicate a need for an additional investment in assets (especially fixed assets) or a need to slow growth. If sales are disproportionately low, there is the possible existence of under-utilized assets which should be sold. The sales/fixed assets ratio and the accounts receivable and inventory turn ratios may be helpful in analyzing the sales/assets relationship in more depth.

Ratio relationships

Although each of these four ratios is individually significant, the analyst should realize how they are interrelated. Because they are tied so closely together, a change in one has implications for the others. This is important in understanding the chain of events scenario which was mentioned in the introduction to Chapter 2 on problem loan detection. In other words, a weakness in one aspect of a company's operations has an impact on other areas and starts a chain of events which, if not interrupted, leads to serious financial difficulties.

To understand the interrelationships consider sales/assets as a starting point. If sales grow, so too must assets. As assets grow, debt must increase to finance them. The increase in debt affects the profit/debt relationship, so profit must grow to maintain the ratio. The relationship between sales and expenses has an impact on profits which in turn influences the profit/debt ratio. The debt/equity ratio was affected by both the increase in debt and the profits.

This example illustrates how closely related each of these ratios is and the importance of assuring that they are in sync individually and as a whole. These relationships comprise the foundation of the company's financial structure. They assure basic long-range financial stability.

Break-even analysis

In simplest terms, break-even represents that level of sales at which total revenues equal total costs. There are three factors which influence a company's break-even:

1. Variable costs. Those which vary with sales or volume, such as raw materials and sales commissions.

2. Fixed costs. Those which do not vary with sales, for example, overhead.

3. Price

Break-even can be expressed as a formula: $B/E = \dfrac{FC}{1 - VC}$

B/E = break-even sales ($).

FC = fixed costs ($).

VC = variable costs (%).

$1 - VC$ is called the contribution margin. It is that portion of each sales dollar that is left after variable costs have been covered. For example, if VC equals 60% then 40% of each sales dollar is available to cover fixed costs. Since variable costs are expressed as a percentage of sales, the variable cost percentage can be affected by a change in price.

With a knowledge of fixed and variable costs, a company's break-even sales ($) can be calculated. This alone can be helpful because it tells how much sales increase is necessary to reach break-even or how far sales can slide before the company loses money. The break-even formula has three additional uses:

1. If the break-even sales level is known, the balance-sheet structure needed to support that level of sales can be calculated. From this, debt levels and capital adequacy can be determined. Bear in mind that payments of principal of long-term debt will be amortized from after-tax profit and are not included in the break-even calculation. Consequently, any long-term debt which is projected on the break-even balance sheet has to be paid from profits as sales exceed break-even.

2. The formula can be solved for any variable—sales, fixed costs, or variable costs. For example, if variable costs are known and the level of sales can be projected with accuracy, the formula can be solved for fixed costs. This indicates the level of fixed costs which the company can support. The same could be done for variable costs.

3. An additional use for the break-even formula is sensitivity analysis. The assumption about any one of the variables, sales, fixed or variable costs can easily be altered and the impact measured. For example, if management's projections indicate fixed costs of $500,000 with VC at 65%, then B/E = $1,111,111. If the bank is more comfortable with an assumption of FC at $600,000, then the resulting B/E = $1,333.333. This new break-even sales level results in a different balance-sheet structure since higher sales means increased inventory and accounts receivable and greater financial requirements.

Operating leverage

The understanding of a company's cost structure gained from break-even analysis is also helpful in projecting the impact of a change in sales volume on profitability. If the major portion of costs are fixed, then as sales increase, costs will remain nearly the same and profits will multiply as sales exceed break-even. Alternatively, if sales decrease, fixed costs will not keep pace and losses will mount as sales levels drop below break-even.

The greater the fixed component of costs, the greater the operating leverage and the more rapid the increase in profitability above break-even. High operating leverage equates with a high contribution margin in the break-even formula. For example, if fixed costs as a percent of total costs are high, variable costs will be low. The result is that more of each sales dollar will be available after the fixed costs are met. If VC = 50%, then 50¢ on each dollar is available for profits after fixed costs are covered. If VC = 25¢, then 75% of each dollar will go to profit.

When devising a workout plan, an understanding of operating leverage is invaluable. It suggests that a company with high operating leverage stands to suffer significant losses if sales drop below break-even. Consequently, the options are to lower the break-even or find a way to increase sales. The company with low operating leverage can reduce sales and shrink the company without suffering the same magnitude of losses, because costs are primarily variable. However, an increase in sales will not result in a significant improvement in profit. The best option for a company with this type of cost structure is to reduce sales. The knowledge of a company's cost structure can be used in conjunction with working investment analysis to provide an even clearer picture of the options in a workout.

Working investment analysis

Working assets and liabilities are those which increase or decrease proportionately with a change in sales, for example, accounts receivable, inventory, accounts payable, and accruals. An increase in working assets is financed primarily from an increase in working liabilities. Any shortfall must be financed by other sources, specifically debt or equity.

Working investment (WI) represents the difference in working assets (accounts receivable and inventory) and working liabilities (accounts payable and accruals). It is the amount which must be financed by other sources. The amount of the working investment can be related to sales to derive the working investment factor. For example:

Accounts Receivable	$200,000
Inventory	+ 400,000
Working Assets	$600,000

Accounts Payable	$160,000
Accruals	+40,000
Working Liabilities	$200,000

Working Assets	$600,000
Working Liabilities	−200,000
Working Investment	$400,000

Sales = $2,000,000. Therefore, working investment factor (WIF) = 400,000/2,000,000 = 20%

This factor represents the amount to be financed from outside sources expressed as a percentage of sales. Assuming inventory, accounts receivable, and accounts payable turns remain constant, the WIF can be applied to any projected level of sales to determine financing requirements. For example:

Projected Sales = $3,000,000
WI = 20% (WIF) × $3,000,000 = $600,000
Previous WI = $400,000

An additional $200,000 must be financed by debt or equity. If profits equal $200,000 and are not already committed to amortize existing debt, or for capital expenditures, or other purposes, then no outside financing will be required. From the example, it is deduced that the higher the working investment factor, the greater the need for financing to support working assets.

As mentioned, the concepts of operating leverage and working investment can be combined to derive options for financing workouts. If a company combines a low WIF with high operating leverage, an increase in sales will:

• Require minimal financing to support working assets.
• Generate significant profits above break-even.

If a company combines high WIF with low operating leverage, a decrease in sales will:

• Generate significant cash from liquidation of working assets which can be used to reduce long-term debt or as a cash cushion.
• Result in lower costs as sales decrease (since costs are variable) and limit losses.

By reversing the logic, a company with low WIF and high operating leverage which attempted to lower sales would find losses mounting rapidly with little cash from asset liquidation as an offset. The company with high WIF and low operating leverage would face increasing financing requirements to support working assets with little help from added profits.

The selection of options in drafting a workout plan should consider the unique features and structure of the company's balance sheet and income statement. However, this information must be integrated into the information about other factors affecting the company, such as competition, market demand, and price elasticity. Even though an increase in sales may be the option indicated by analysis, it may not be feasible in a recessionary economy.

Analysis of Other Factors

So far, the discussion of analysis has centered on the crucial areas of management and financial performance. These are internal factors which must be considered in virually every problem loan situation. However, there are many other areas which could be crucial to a determination of causes or the development of solutions. Some of those which are of greatest importance include the company's product and physical plant, which are additional internal factors, and the market, industry, and economy, which are external factors.

Internal Factors

Among the product considerations:

- Is the product a consumer or durable good or is a service provided?
- Is it perishable or durable?
- Is its demand elastic or inelastic? Are sales fad- or style-related?
- Is there a technical obsolescence factor?
- What is the product's life cycle and where on the cycle is it located?
- Is there a diverse product mix or a single product?

Physical plant and production considerations include:

- Condition of existing plant? Is there need for improvements, repairs, or additions?
- What is capacity utilization of existing plant?
- Replacement costs of property, plant, and equipment?
- Relative efficiency of plant and production process? What is technological status—current with industry or obsolete?
- Automation of plant relative to industry?
- Labor- or capital-intensive production process?
- Seasonal or level production?
- Salability of plant and equipment? Prospective buyers/users and general demand for this type facility?
- Is company production/quality oriented? Company's success based on quality or uniqueness and availability of product?

External Factors

There are three areas which fall in this category.

1. Economic Considerations

- General business conditions? Impact on company of economic fluctuations, recession?
- Impact on customers and suppliers of economic fluctuations?
- Susceptibility to interest rates?
- Regional economic dependence and economic base of region, for example, concentrated in aerospace, auto industry, etc.?
- Susceptibility to foreign exchange rates and value of dollar? Susceptibility to internationsl or foreign economies?
- Susceptibility to stock or bond market fluctuations?

2. Industry Considerations

- Composition of industry—dominated by large companies or composed of numerous small- or medium-size companies?
- Ease of entry?
- General health of industry as determined by growth rate, failure rate, and profitability?
- Is industry highly competitive with prospects of shake-out? Is industry young and growing, established and stable, stagnant, or on the decline?
- Who are industry leaders? What is position of company within the industry?
- Is industry seasonal, cyclical, countercyclical?
- Is industry capital- or labor-intensive?
- What is impact of government regulations? Is industry regulated or deregulated?
- Is industry unionized? What has been history of union relations, strikes, etc.? What has been the impact of strikes, labor cost increases, or other union demands?

3. Market Considerations

- Composition of the market—diversified with many customers or concentrated with several large customers?
- Financial strength of customers?
- Profile of customer base—geographical distribution, age, income, and other demographics?
- Potential impact of changing sociological trends such as age composition of populace in the geographical market?
- Profile of competitors? Sales size, marketing strategy, financial condition, market share?
- Market share controlled by company?

- Importance of changing consumer preferences or buying patterns? Condos instead of houses or apartments, for example.
- Is company sales- and marketing-oriented? Success depends on the ability to sell, rather than on the ability to provide a unique product or service.
- What is company's niche and marketing strategy?
- Are advertising/marketing firms used or is marketing function in-house? Is radio, TV, newspaper, billboard, or direct mail used?
- What method of sales and distribution? Direct sales using salesmen? Distributors or brokers? Wholesalers or catalog sales?

This does not exhaust all the possible factors which may require analysis in a problem loan situation. However, it covers some of the major areas which should be explored both to determine causes and as a prerequisite to the design of a long-range plan of corporate rehabilitation.

The Emergency Plan

When a company experiences the advanced stages of a cash crisis, there is a high probability that cash-out is exceeding cash-in. Obviously this condition cannot persist or the company will be broke. However, it frequently takes time to move from the detection phase in problem loans to the development and implementation of a long-range turnaround plan. When turnaround is the best alternative, there must be an emergency, short-term plan to "stop the bleeding." Measures should be taken to ensure positive cash generation to buy the necessary time to develop and implement the long-range plan.

Elements

Basically, the steps to improve the company's cash situation fall into three categories: cost cutting, revenue generation, and the sale of assets. The elements of the emergency plan will vary from company to company and probably entail some of the following:

- Quickly getting control over key control items.
- Sell unneeded assets.
- Cut back on staff and salaries.
- Reduce R&D.
- Cut capital expenditures.
- Restructure debt on longer terms.
- Refinance assets—buildings.
- Sale and leaseback of assets.
- Reduce inventory levels.
- Speed accounts receivable collections.

- Develop a plan for paying the trade more slowly or with partial payments.
- Reduce pension accruals.
- Eliminate "perks."
- Write-down inventory or other assets to receive tax benefits.
- Close or sell plants or subsidiaries that are cash users rather than generators.
- Eliminate products or territories which are unprofitable or marginally profitable but require support in the form of staff or inventory.

Clearly, these are emergency measures which are not to be pursued frivolously but only after reasonable analysis to determine the benefits versus the costs. This analysis requires the kind of detailed breakout of cash flows into and out of the business, which is found in a cash budget. The usual cash budget is helpful in identifying major uses for cash, but a further breakout may be necessary to determine which territories or products are cash users versus cash providers. After the plan has been decided, the company's general cash budget will have to be recast to determine:

- How much time has been bought.
- When cash flow from operations will again become positive.
- Any shortfall that may have to be financed by other means. For example, additional bank borrowings, principals contribution, outside investors, and so on.

Long-Range Rehabilitation Strategy

Although the previously described elements of the emergency plan help bridge the period from crises to solution, they can also be incorporated into a long-term rehabilitation strategy. Regardless of the source of a company's problems, there will eventually be financial implications. Consequently, there almost always will be a significant effort to realign the company financially so that the structure is compatible with the new company which emerges from the rehabilitation. The financial adjustments are designed to increase cash inflow and reduce cash outflow. Outflow is affected by reductions in costs or by reducing or restructuring debt. Inflow is enhanced by generating additional revenue or by changing the components of the operating cycle—carrying fewer days of inventory or accounts receivable.

These financial measures are intended to restore viability by changing the company's break-even and returning cash flow to a positive state. In the chapter introduction, the additional requirements for viability were stated as competent management and a sound strategy based on analysis conclusions. The design of strategy depends on an accurate evaluation of causes. However, judging strategy set by others may be difficult for the banker. If strategy entails specialized or technical expertise, such as changes in marketing methods or product design, the banker may be on unsure ground. However, there are five guidelines that should be applied in judging strategy:

1. Is it logical? Does it make sense to the layman? Is the strategy clear in its conception?

2. Can it be done? Is there a plan for execution that has been thoroughly developed with resources, assignments, and deadlines established?

3. Can it be interpreted in terms of financial results? Are the results acceptable to the banker in terms of the bank's involvement and risk?

4. Does it make sense to others such as consultants or those knowledgeable in the industry?

5. Is management capable of pulling it off? Without the ability to become totally comfortable with the strategy, it is essential that there be great faith in management.

Summary

Analyzing a problem loan can be loosely compared with solving a jigsaw puzzle. However, there are some additional complications. First, the pieces have to be found before they can be put together. To further complicate things, the puzzle changes constantly and rarely do the pieces fit perfectly to form a clear picture. Also, there are time limits on the construction, and there are many more pieces available than are needed. Finally, the puzzle owner constantly provides erroneous clues.

When as many of the information pieces are found as possible, given time constraints, analysis begins. In this phase, the analyst attempts to determine what is relevant and how all the pieces fit together. The problem puzzle includes pieces of information on management, financial performance, the economy, the industry, the market, and other factors. They are all gathered and analyzed to see if there is a thread or several threads which emerge. This enables the analyst to focus on those pieces of information which are most relevant.

When there are enough clues, the puzzle takes sufficient shape to allow some conclusions to be drawn about problems and possible solutions. Next, the process of using the information to formulate a plan of action begins.

Developing the Game Plan 5

As the banker begins to develop the workout game plan, he or she should recognize that there are generally several available options. These options may range from doing nothing to demanding payment, to liquidating collateral, to petitioning to put the borrower into an involuntary bankruptcy.

In considering the available options, one should not lose sight of the proposition that the game plan is for the bank *not* the borrower. The banker obviously needs to present the chosen plan to the borrower in such a manner that the borrower accepts the plan as being in his or her best interest as well as the bank's. This is simply a matter of negotiating. It is obviously desirable for the debtor to be totally rehabilitated and for other creditors to be repaid as much as possible. But these are secondary to the objective of the bank getting paid out.

Anticipating the Possible Stages to Payout

In considering the development of a game plan to collect a problem loan, it is helpful to look at the possible stages to payout. Obviously, many problem loans never go through all or even most of the possible stages. Most bankers hope that they will move from credit discomfort into the workout stage and then straight from the workout stage to payout. Fortunately, this often happens. In many other problem loans, however, it does not happen, and the path from workout to payout involves several steps. A complete understanding of the later stages and the problems that may be confronted in them assists the bank in developing a more successful game plan. It is helpful to look at the possible stages to payout in the following format:

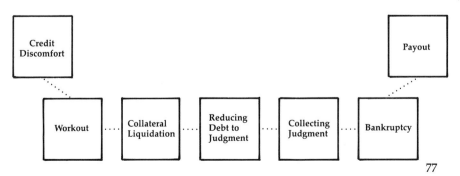

Workout

Workout is sometimes used to include the entire subject of problem loans including litigation and bankruptcy stages. As used here, workout means the cooperative, voluntary agreement between bank and debtor to establish a framework for the repayment of the indebtedness. The bank and the debtor may determine that it is in both their interests to handle the debt by agreement, without resort to foreclosure, legal action, or bankruptcy. While workout may entail varying degrees of cooperation, intimidation, and mutual concessions, it often appears to both parties as an alternative preferable to those later stages in the problem loan cycle.

Collateral Liquidation

Collateral liquidation, described in greater detail in Chapter 7, is the process of converting the collateral given by the debtor to secure the indebtedness into cash for application against the debt owed to the bank. Depending on the amount of collateral originally given to secure the debt and the success in liquidating it, the bank may still be left with debt owing, even after collateral liquidation has been completed.

Reducing the Debt to Judgment

The bank may never have had any collateral. It may have liquidated the collateral and still have a deficiency. For strategic reasons, it may have determined to defer collateral liquidation until a later day. In any event, the bank has debt owing, and it determines to obtain a judgment against some party who is liable for the debt, either the maker of its note or a guarantor.

The process of reducing the debt to judgment begins with the filing of a complaint in either a state or federal court. It concludes with the court's adjudication that the bank is entitled to a sum certain from the maker or the guarantor. This adjudication is called the judgment, and the process and difficulties of obtaining a judgment are described in Chapter 8.

Collection of the Judgment

Once the bank has obtained a judgment, the process of collecting the judgment ensues. The judgment may either be paid voluntarily or payment may be obtained involuntarily through use of one or more of the postjudgment remedies discussed in Chapter 9.

Bankruptcy

Often, one of the earlier stages in the problem loan cycle such as collateral liquidation or collection of the judgment precipitates either a voluntary or an involuntary filing by the debtor, seeking to obtain protection under one of the chapters of the bankruptcy law. The bankruptcy stage is treated in Chapters 10 through 14.

Preliminary Considerations

Borrower's Ability to Move the Debt

The bank should always consider the ability of the borrower to move the debt. It is surprising how often a bank's bad loan is one that took out another bank. If the bank identifies the problem soon enough and quietly enough, it is possible that some other lender, in haste for loan production, may miss some of the warning signs and make the loan that takes the first bank out. Obviously, the bank must be astute to distinguish between the true problem loan and the fast-growing company that has and should be expected to have a tight cash flow. These companies are the truly profitable bank customers today and may be the bank's largest and most solid relationships tomorrow. The bank should be careful in its haste to run off problems not to run off some of its most profitable relationships.

Bank's Tolerance for Problems

Different banks have varying degrees of tolerance for dealing with problem loans. The same bank's tolerance for dealing with problems may change from time to time. If a bank has few problem loans and strong earnings, then it may be able to afford the luxury of working with a borrower over an extended period of time. If the bank has a significant number of problems, even though the bank might get more actual dollars back on a present value basis, the bank may be better served by getting as much back as possible in the short run and getting over one more problem. This is sometimes seen in the extreme. A bank will write down every problem loan during one quarter, suffer the immediate earnings problem, and then get on with its business. Therefore, an early item on the agenda for the workout officer is to understand the attitude and condition of the bank and its tolerance for protracted workouts.

The Bank's Collateral Cushion or Shortfall

The bank should evaluate its collateral position, comparing the liquidation value of its collateral against the indebtedness of the borrower. The difference is either the bank's cushion or its shortfall. When there is a collateral cushion, the bank should consider how long it is likely to take to effect a successful workout and the degree to which the collateral cushion may become impaired. Where there is already a collateral shortfall, the bank must make its best judgment about the long-term viability of the borrower and whether there is sufficient potential earning capacity to pay the bank out. If the bank has a collateral cushion, but the cushion and the borrower's financial condition are deteriorating, the bank may want to demand payment or liquidate its collateral position rather than move into some prolonged workout.

Renewal: The Quick Fix

Bankers sometimes are criticized for simply renewing a note. Renewal is sometimes equated with either a refusal to recognize the problem or a refusal to grapple with it once it has been recognized. However, a renewal can be a legitimate, short-term game plan. Renewal for a short period permits the bank and the debtor to evaluate the loan and possible alternatives for a longer term rework. The renewal can also be an opportunity to correct collateral deficiencies that may have surfaced in the loan. If, for example, the banker is aware that he or she has failed to obtain a security agreement, a financing statement, or some other collateral document necessary to complete the collateral package, then the bank can use the renewal to correct the documentation deficiency.

Finally and perhaps most important, it is the law in most jurisdictions that renewal of a note cuts off all defenses of which the maker has knowledge at the time of renewal. For example, if the debtor contends that execution of the original note was somehow without consideration or the result of fraud but, nevertheless, executes a renewal note, the renewal note constitutes a waiver of all the debtor's then-known defenses. Thus, renewal of the note may perform a legitimate, short-term workout function.

When Discounting Looks Good

Sometimes even the most thorough analysis leads to the conclusion that a problem is insoluble. When that is the case, one needs to consider getting out while it is still possible, even if it means discounting the debt. In many instances, one lender has taken another lender out of a credit, only to find the borrower in bankruptcy in 12 to 18 months. Occasionally, salvation comes in the form of the greater fool. By refusing to rework a loan and by being generally intractable, a loan officer can encourage the borrower to move the debt. An offer to compromise the interest owing may get a borrower to try all avenues to move the debt and effect the interest savings. Moreover, if the bank officer probably will not get that interest in the long run, he or she has only given up a problem, not interest income.

Therefore, when evaluating game plans, the loan officer should always consider the nature of the problem, whether or not the borrower can truly be rehabilitated, the time and expense of so doing, and the potential for expensive litigation, before moving into the workout stage. The bank and the borrower may often both be best served with a cut-and-run solution. If the bank officer is convinced that the situation is hopeless, maybe the borrower can be persuaded to liquidate, getting the bank out on some discounted basis, and perhaps even preserving something for the debtor. On occasion, a quick cut and run makes a lot of sense.

Preparing the Wish List

Earlier we discussed the importance of thoroughly reviewing the bank's credit files, collateral files, and public records. From this review, the banker should have obtained a good understanding of the history of the customer relationship, the problems and complaints that surfaced during the relationship, the collateral held by the bank, and how the bank fits into the borrower's overall debt picture. This understanding enables the bank to prepare its wish list.

What is the wish list? It is a compilation of all those items which, with the benefit of hindsight, the bank would want if it could start all over again and structure the loan anew.

Think about it in the abstract. Write down all the items that you wish that the bank had gotten in the beginning! Does the bank have a properly perfected position on all inventory, accounts receivable, and equipment? Does the bank have a lien on the actual physical facilities or a landlord's waiver? How about personal guarantees?

Are the guarantees collateralized? Does the bank have a lien on the principal's personal residence? Who owns residence? Does the owner of the residence guarantee the indebtedness? Are there related companies? Does the bank have the guarantee of those companies?

How about negative pledges? Is there a restriction on the upstreaming of dividends to a parent company? Would you now have priced the loan differently? Are all loans to the borrower cross-defaulted and cross-collateralized? In summary, write down all the various aspects of buttoning up the loan that could have been done in the beginning but were not done. Why do this now when the horse appears to be about out of the barn? Simply to prepare for the next negotiating session with a borrower. This is the first step in being prepared to meet the borrower.

Sometimes workout manuals and handouts suggest that the first things the banker should do when confronted with a problem loan is to visit the borrower, impress on him or her the seriousness of the situation, and to strive to reach some resolution of the problem. This can often be a foolhardy move if the banker is not thoroughly prepared for the meeting. Unless the banker has done his or her homework prior to visiting the borrower, the banker may either make statements that he or she may later come to regret, make tentative suggestions that are later alleged to be firm agreements, or in some other way further imperil the bank's position. This leads to the next step in preparing for the game plan, namely, the preliminary definition of the problem, from the perspective of both the bank and the borrower.

Relative Strengths and Weaknesses

An analysis of the parties' respective strengths and weaknesses is necessary if one is to adequately prepare the game plan. It may be helpful to prepare four separate lists:

1. Lender's strengths and how to capitalize on them.
2. Lender's weaknesses and how to shore them up.
3. Borrower's strengths and how to use and/or negate them.
4. Borrower's weaknesses and how to use and/or shore them up.

Lender's Strengths

Generally, the bank has good documents. Its note forms and collateral documents are typically the product of years of careful drafting and revision. Unless the bank for some reason has permitted the debtor's counsel to prepare the loan documents, it should start out with a strong documentation package which clearly spells out the bank's rights and the borrower's obligations. Generally, the law protects the bank's right to repayment of its principal with interest and perhaps its collection costs. Finally, the bank has the resources, both in money and experienced counsel, to engage, if necessary, in protracted negotiation and litigation. A banker should be aware of these strengths and not hesitate to use them to best advantage.

Lender's Weaknesses

The lender's weaknesses should be fairly easy to enumerate after completion of the review of the bank's files and public records. Other sections of this book have dealt in detail with review of these files and records, and what to look for: proper documentation or lack thereof, other lenders and their collateral position, federal and state tax liens, pending litigation against the debtor, ambiguous loan agreements, letters to or from the debtor that could be interpreted as giving rise to debtor defenses, possibly fraudulent conveyances of assets by the debtor, and the like.

If lender weaknesses are discovered, the account officer should discuss with counsel the best way to correct them. Sometimes, loan renewal wipes out those defenses as to which the borrower either has or ought to have knowledge. Collateral documentation deficiencies or filing errors can often be corrected if caught in time. As long as the relationship between bank and borower is still being handled amicably, many lender weaknesses can be shored up with a minimum of bank concessions. This suggests the importance of thorough preparation before the bank and borrower have gotten into direct confrontation.

Borrower Strengths

One of the major strengths of the borrower is that generally the banker cannot best resolve a problem loan without the cooperation of the borrower. Sometimes this cooperation must be prodded, but it is generally necessary. An unnecessarily tough approach by the bank can make future cooperation more difficult. The too aggressive bank sometimes has the opportunity of having its customer and its collateral languish in the bankruptcy court for several years while its loan is absolutely nonperforming. This experience is often sufficient to impress the banker with the preferability of trying in the future to solve the problem by working with the borrower. The lesson sometimes is learned too late.

This is not to suggest that the banker should be petrified at the prospect of a bankruptcy. It is only to sugget that the most pleasant litigation and bankruptcy experiences are often those that were avoided.

Other strengths of the borrower are obviously the inverse of the lender's weaknesses. If the lender's weaknesses can be eliminated prior to a breakdown in communications and hardening of positions, the bank may get the weaknesses eliminated before the borrower realizes many of his or her strengths. The borrower may also have important financial strengths such as an essentially sound business, unencumbered assets, the ability to raise additional capital, available guarantors, and the ability to move the indebtedness to some other lender.

Borrower's Weaknesses

The borrower's weaknesses may be substantial. Primary among the weaknesses is that he or she has borrowed the money and is obligated to repay it. Typically, the borrower needs financial concessions and may not have the financial strength for protracted conflict with the bank. One loan, even a large one, in bankruptcy or litigation should not seriously imperil the viability of the bank, but the borrower may not be able to say the same thing. The borrower frequently stands to lose everything that he or she may have worked a lifetime to accumulate. The most primary needs are security and survival. When faced with their possible loss, the borrower may be willing to perform most reasonable requests to ensure survival.

This survival instinct obviously can cut both ways. The borrower's memory may be affected as to conversations held with the account officer. The borrower may transfer assets in order to protect them or may even lie, steal, and cheat. The tone set by the bank can determine whether the borrower's survival instincts are channeled toward goals that are ultimately beneficial to the bank. Cornering the borrower may make for a satisfied banker but also can create a desperate and dangerous borrower.

Two other important borrower weaknesses are the objectivity and clarity with which the borrower is able to view the situation. Particularly in the early stages of a problem loan, the borrower may be more optimistic than is warranted. An astute account officer can take advantage of this optimism by not preaching doom and gloom. He or she can agree to assist the borrower through this "temporary" problem and condition the assistance on needed borrower concessions.

Analytical Process

Developing the game plan is an analytical process that should always precede action. *Think; then act.* Frequently, particularly with less-experienced bankers, problem loans get one of two possible reactions: the first is the "ostrich" syndrome. If you ignore the problem, it will go away. The second reaction is the reverse of the first. The banker immediately jumps on the problem with both feet without doing his or her homework.

Unnecessary haste and inadequate preparation can lead to an ordinary problem becoming a serious misadventure. For example, a large bank had a problem loan with a manufacturing company. The company's assets, in addition to inventory and accounts receivable, consisted of heavy equipment and large overhead cranes used in lifting and moving inventory in a building owned by a party closely related to the debtor. In addition, there was a fleet of off-road cranes used in the installation of the fabricated product. When the problem surfaced, the bank jumped in aggressively, declaring the loan in default and commencing to foreclose on the collateral. Predictably, the borrower filed a Chapter 11 petition.

The bankruptcy judge ruled that the large overhead cranes, which could be physically removed from the real estate, were nonetheless fixtures. Since there was no landlord's waiver, the bank was not entitled to them. Furthermore, the bank's security interest in the off-road cranes (used for years, on and off the road, without being titled as motor vehicles) was held not to have been properly perfected by a Uniform Commercial Code filing. The court held that the bank should have filed as with motor vehicles. Thus, the cranes became the property of the estate to be disposed of for the benefit of general creditors. These two problems, which could have been easily averted early in a workout, resulted in the bank's suffering a self-inflicted wound which cost hundreds of thousands of dollars.

Summary

The game plan is needed to solve a financial problem. In formulating the game plan, one should not lose sight that a financial problem generally must have a financial solution. Problems sometimes take on lives of their own. Both the borrower and the banker have reputations at stake and pride on the line. Lawyers may enter the picture who have little knowledge of or interest in the core financial problem. They may seek to enhance their reputations by exercises involving playing on their clients' concerns over reputation and pride.

Rather than formulating constructive game plans to solve financial problems, both sides engage in feverish searches for negotiation and litigation weapons. The borrower and the borrower's attorney look for weaknesses in the bank's collateral position to exploit, for some written evidence of a promise to renew the loan or commit to advance new funds, or for some evidence of bank officer misconduct.

The bank and its attorney pore over old financial statements to see whether the borrower either misrepresented its financial condition or transferred assets to defraud the bank. They review collateral records to see whether the same collateral has been pledged to more than one creditor or may have been disposed of without the proceeds having been applied to the bank's debt. They search for evidence of the borrower's officers' and principals' having bled it of funds that otherwise should have been used to repay the bank debt.

In short, the issue moves from addressing the core financial problem to obtaining negotiation or litigation leverage. In the process, a solvable problem may grow into an unsolvable morass, and the well of trust and cooperation between bank and borrower may be permanently poisoned.

None of this suggests that the bank should not prepare itself for those fights ultimately to be fought. It is to suggest that particularly in the initial stages of planning, it is important that the banker and the bank's attorney not lose sight of the core financial problem.

Deciding on Workout 6

Workout was defined in the previous chapter as the cooperative, voluntary agreement between bank and borrower to establish a framework for the repayment of indebtedness. The primary purpose of workout is to obtain payment of the indebtedness owed to the bank while minimizing some of those costs typically associated with problem loans.

Purposes of Workout

Obviously, even before workout, the bank had the debtor's promise to pay in the form of its original note. Why substitute a new promise to pay for the old one? Something must be obtained in the process that improves the likelihood of repayment or eliminates some of the potential costs in order to make it worth the bank's while to enter into a workout agreement. The purposes which the bank should seek to achieve in the workout phase are discussed in the following paragraphs.

Improving the Bank's Documentation

If the bank determines that it has collateral documents improperly executed, lost or missing, or containing erroneous or incomplete collateral descriptions, or any other documentation deficiencies, the bank may well conclude that a workout phase to correct the documentation deficiencies is preferable to having the deficiencies exposed during collateral liquidation. The banker, with the assistance of legal counsel, should determine precisely what additional documentation may be needed and what corrective steps may be required to perfect the documentation in hand. The bank should then use the workout phase to condition any concessions it may make on the completing or correcting of deficiencies in its collateral package.

Taking Additional Collateral

Often the documentation on existing collateral is in good order, but there are items of collateral which would strengthen the bank's position but were not taken when the loan was originally made. These might include a personal guarantee by a principal, a security interest in unencumbered collateral, a subordinate security interest in encumbered collateral,

collateral available from guarantors, estoppel letters from the holders of prior security interests, and innumerable other items which the bank may now wish to obtain. The bank should use the workout phase to condition any concessions it may make on the debtor's providing it with these additional items of collateral.

Eliminating Debtor Defenses

During the course of reviewing the bank's file or discussions with the customer, the bank may have determined that there are potential debtor defenses (see Chapter 8) which have some possible basis in fact. The bank should use the workout phase to condition any concessions it may make on a waiver of defenses and a release of any claims which the debtor may have against the bank.

Playing on Debtor Optimism

If the bank has recognized its problem early enough, then its debtor may still be quite optimistic about its long-term prospects. If the problem is not yet acute, the debtor will typically rationalize it as resulting from general market conditions, temporary cash flow problems, the weather, a strike, management changes, a new computer, and as many possible excuses as the rationalizing mind can conceive. In most cases, the debtor truly believes and tries to convince the bank that the problem identified by the banker is either totally nonexistent or, at worst, temporary.

The banker should utilize the workout phase to play on this very real debtor optimism. Sales are always going to be higher next month; the big deal is going to close early next quarter; the debtor's ship is about to come in. The banker's workout plan should be built on the foundation of the debtor's optimism. If the debtor says he or she cannot pay the seasonal line off in March but can pay it out over April, May, and June, then build that commitment into the workout agreement. If the debtor is unable to reduce the line as promised because the inventory is 20% higher than projected but says that a sale will reduce the inventory to the projected levels in 60 days, build that into the workout program. The optimistic debtor can be a very helpful partner in putting together the basic outline of the workout agreement.

Positioning for Later Stages

Most important, the workout phase should always involve a forward look through those possible stages discussed in the payout format in Chapter 5. The banker should anticipate the problems likely to be confronted during collateral liquidation, during reducing the debt to judgment, during trying to collect the judgment, and perhaps even in bankruptcy. If collateral liquidation will eventually be a problem because the collateral will be subject to the rent claim of the debtor's landlord, then condition any concessions on the debtor's obtaining a waiver of the landlord's rights as part of the workout agreement.

If obtaining a judgment will be difficult because of possible debtor defenses and a litigious debtor, then condition workout concessions on language whereby the debtor acknowledges the debt, waives defenses, and releases the bank from possible counterclaims. If the banker is concerned about an ability to collect a judgment because the debtor probably will transfer his or her remaining assets before the bank obtains judgment, then use workout to obtain liens on those additional assets which may later be needed to satisfy a possible judgment.

There are two basic rules of workout:

1. If you cannot improve your position in workout, you should not be there.

2. Never give anything away. Trade up!

Specific Workout Problems to Avoid

Chapter 8 lists some 15 issues that can give rise to either debtor defenses or counterclaims. The bank should obviously avoid taking action during workout which may give rise to any possible liability under any of these issues. In addition, there are a number of other potential legal pitfalls to which the bank should be alert.

Environmental Problems

The past few years have witnessed the enactment of a substantial body of both state and federal law designed to protect the environment. These laws are administered by the federal Environmental Protection Agency and similar state agencies. One of the focal points of environmental legislation is hazardous waste disposal and hazardous waste clean up. These laws create potential liability for companies that do not properly dispose of hazardous waste materials. While the laws are aimed at the company that creates the hazardous waste, the company's lender may inadvertently incur liability.

The most likely lender liability arises from laws that give the state environmental agency some superlien against the company's property to secure the site clean-up obligation. The bank that thought it had a first priority lien on its debtor's property may be surprised that its lien has been reduced, or even wiped out, by the debtor's environmental liabilities. A second, but less likely, type of liability is where the lender has arguably participated in the management of the borrower's business. This has prompted some states to try to impose direct liability for clean-up on the lender, unrelated to the question of its collateral and imposing clean-up liens on it.

There are instances in which state and federal environmental officials have asserted claims against banks for the failure of their borrowers to properly clean up hazardous waste. Some of these claims have been settled for medium six-figure amounts. Thus, in workouts involving debtors in environmentally sensitive industries, the bank should be alert to the potential environmental liabilities when it either considers taking back its collateral, either voluntarily or through foreclosure, or taking any other action which may suggest that the bank participated in the management of its debtor.

Pension Problems

In 1974, Congress enacted the Employee Retirement Income Security Act (ERISA). Among other things, ERISA established the Pension Benefit Guaranty Corporation (PBGC). The PBGC was established so that participants in ERISA-covered pension plans would be insured against loss if their pension plans were terminated. Where an employer terminates an underfunded pension plan, PBGC pays the benefits to the employees which would have been paid under the pension plan. In such case, the company which has terminated the plan may become liable to the PBGC for the lesser of the amount by which the value of the guaranteed benefits under the pension plan exceed the value of the plan's assets or 30% of the company's net worth.

Once this liability has been established, the PBGC is granted a lien on all the real and personal property belonging to the employer. While the lien does not take priority over a prior perfected security interest, it would have priority over unsecured advances and new advances made for security taken after the PBGC's lien attached. This problem is aggravated because the PBGC does not file its liens in the public recording files of the various states. The bank may have to inquire about any such lien from the borrower or by directly contacting the PBGC in Washington, D.C.

Tax Problems

Federal law makes a lender potentially liable for the payment of unpaid employment taxes where the lender supplies funds for the borrower's use in paying employee wages. Thus, in any workout situation in which the bank advances funds which may be used to make borrower payroll, the bank should ensure that the borrower makes provision for all required employment taxes.

Bankruptcy Problems

Chapter 10 defines an "insider" for purposes of the Bankruptcy Code and discusses the bank's potential liability if it becomes an insider. An insider includes a "person in control" of the debtor. The preference period for an insider is one year prior to the date of the filing of the bankruptcy petition, as compared with the 90-day period applicable to noninsiders. In addition, an insider found to have abused its relationship may have its claims subordinated to the claims of general creditors. Thus, it is important that the bank carefully avoid clothing itself with rights which might be construed to make it a person in control of the debtor or any role which causes the bank to appear to be managing or directing the affairs of the debtor.

Trade Creditors

In many problem loan situations, there is a debtor; a major bank lender secured by inventory, equipment, and accounts receivable; and a group of unsecured trade creditors ("the trade"). The trade may in the aggregate constitute a significant creditor element. Its individual components may, however, represent small credits. These small creditors may have little comprehension of the magnitude of the debtor's total trade debt. There may be little or no communication or coordination among the individual components of the trade creditor group. Geographically, the trade creditors may be widely dispersed. Often, no one member of the trade creditor group has sufficient exposure and consequent motivation to exercise any leadership role among the trade generally. Often, bank debt is personally guaranteed by principals of the debtor. Rarely is trade debt guaranteed.

This sometime leads to an attitude by the debtor or by the primary bank creditors conducive to the repayment of the bank debt at the expense of the trade. This is sometime referred to as "riding the trade" and can take many forms. It may mean that the debtor that normally has paid the trade within 10 days stretches the payment out to 30, 60 or 90 days and uses the corresponding cash flow to reduce bank debt. On occasion, this may be coupled with significant increases in the volume of inventory or equipment purchased, which may increase the collateral pool available to secured bank creditors.

If the debtor should find itself in a bankruptcy proceeding, the banker should assume that at last the trade will get together in a creditors' committee and perhaps with a trustee. They will review the actions of the debtor and the bank with an attitude which at best will be suspicious and at worst will be hostile.

While the bank is not a fiduciary for the trade, it nevertheless should be extremely attentive to avoid actions which can later be construed as evidencing any conspiracy between the debtor and the bank to take any unfair advantage of the trade. Precautions run the gamut from monitoring the level of trade debt to insisting on workout covenants that assure that the level of trade debt does not rise above agreed levels.

Lending into a Workout

A major rule of workouts ought to be: *Advance new money only as a last resort.* Consider every alternative before advancing new money into a bad situation. There are times when it is appropriate to lend one's way out of a problem, but they are rare. To lend into a bad situation, certain conditions must be met. First, the debtor must have cooperative management that is not part of the problem. The debtor's management must recognize the problem, have the desire and the capability to solve it, and have the incentive to see the problem through to a successful resolution. One easy and true test of the character and commitment of management is willingness to commit additional assets to facilitate the turnaround. This may involve the principal and spouse agreeing to guarantee the loan and collateralizing the guarantee with personal assets. Why should the bank make additional commitments when the principals refuse to do so?

Before advancing new money, the banker must ask whether new money will *improve the bank's position.* If it merely allows the borrower to limp along for a time, then the banker may be simply putting off the inevitable and increasing the bank's exposure.

Reasons to Advance Money

There are at least three valid reasons to advance new money into a troubled situation. The first is to obtain an interest in additional collateral. The banker should be reasonably assured of getting past the preference period. A good rule of thumb is that the new collateral taken should be worth at least twice the amount of the new funds advanced, if the bank is getting a superior lien position. If the bank is getting a junior collateral position, it should advance even less.

A second reason to advance new funds may be to avoid or defer a bankruptcy. Generally, this is to ensure that a preference period passes when the bank has recently received either a significant payment from sources other than its collateral or gotten new collateral worth more than the amount of the bank's advance.

A third reason to advance new money is if the bank's existing collateral position may become worthless without the advance. For example, if a small but prior mortgage is being foreclosed by some other creditor, the bank may have to advance money to pay the small first to protect its substantial secondary collateral position.

Other considerations in any decision to advance new money must include a decision on whether the company is ultimately viable. If the company has been totally shut off by its suppliers, then rehabilitation will be difficult. The bank may not only have to fund advances to pay off the past-due accounts payable but may have to advance money so the borrower can buy new inventory cash on delivery.

In addition, the banker must determine that the problem is readily solvable, and more important, that the company has a good product to sell and a good market to sell it in. If these conditions cannot be met, the banker is probably just delaying the inevitable.

Repayment Source

The most important element of the decision to advance new money must be an *identifiable source of repayment*. If the bank is to put out new money, an unimpeachable source of repayment must be clearly identified. There are all too many examples available in the charge-off files of banks around the U.S. of this rule being violated.

Any time the decision is made to lend new money into a bad situation, certain potential hazards are possible. One hazard is that the new funds will use up the borrowing capacity of the company, the leverage will increase, and the chances of finding another lender will diminish. Perhaps a more important consideration is that the funds advanced should be used to restore the normal funds flow through the business, for example, to keep trade payables within acceptable limits to ensure continued trade support. If the funds are going to be siphoned off for any other reason, then such funds should not be advanced. When the loan reaches this stage, the bank may advance new funds only by check on a joint check basis, that is, to the debtor and the account payable, or the debtor and the Internal Revenue Service.

The banker should remember that new debt means additional debt service, which further restricts the flow of funds for normal operations and reduces financial flexibility. Before advancing new funds, the banker and the borrower should explore other alternatives such as trying to compromise or stretch out repayment of trade debt. The decision to lend into a workout should not be made lightly or before considering all other possibilities.

Liquidating the Collateral 7

For years bankers have been taught the importance of the five Cs of credit: character, capacity, capital, conditions, and collateral. While there can be no substitute for character, collateral may serve to substitute for the other elements. Often, the most direct route from credit discomfort to payout is through the liquidation of collateral. It is the fortunate banker who finds his or her loan sufficiently well collateralized so it is unnecessary to consider any workout solution other than collateral liquidation.

Reviewing Collateral and Ensuring Its Perfection

One of the tasks that should be undertaken in every problem loan is reviewing the collateral held and ensuring that it is properly perfected. Listing the collateral is generally a simple task. In addition to those items of collateral mentioned in the collateral documents, the bank may also have interests in other collateral. The note probably gives the bank a security interest in all accounts and deposits maintained by the debtor with the bank.

There may be collateral documents given to the bank by guarantors on debt unrelated to the borrower's obligation which contain "other indebtedness" language. This language is sometimes referred to as "dragnet" or "open-end" language. It has the effect of taking collateral given for a specific obligation and having it stand for all obligations of the debtor to the bank, including indirect and contingent obligations, such as those incurred by a guarantor.

The bank's direct collateral documents should be reviewed to ensure that the bank has an interest not simply in the collateral stated but also in the proceeds of such collateral. The bank should carefully review the descriptions on its collateral documents to ensure that the bank in fact has what it thinks it has. The bank may think that it has certain equipment which is identified by serial numbers, but finds that the serial numbers on its collateral documents are different from the numbers on the equipment.

There can be disputes over whether general collateral descriptions include particular items of equipment pledged to some other creditor under a more specific description. Even where the bank has a blanket security interest in inventory and other collateral, certain of the collateral may be subject to perfected purchase money security interests of other creditors.

Perfection Problems

Except in rare instances, it is relatively easy to determine what collateral the bank holds. In most cases, it is also easy to determine whether the bank is perfected. Personal property will be perfected by filing in accordance with the provisions of local law. Some states have county filing; others have centralized filing. Common problems likely to jeopardize the bank's security interest in personal property include:

- Failure to file.
- Filing in the wrong county.
- Filing a financing statement on collateral not covered by the underlying security agreement or having property on the underlying security agreement which is not included in the description of the collateral on the financing statement.
- Having the filed financing statement lapse.

The perfection of a collateral interest in real estate is peculiarly a matter of state law. Generally, the mortgage, security deed, or deed of trust is recorded in the county where the property is located. Typically, the filing authorities do not permit the filing of a defective deed. On occasion, however, the filing of a defective deed may result in the bank not perfecting the mortgage, security deed, or deed of trust. This may result from the failure of the deed to be properly notarized or witnessed, the failure of a corporate seal to be affixed, or some other failure under local law. Any question about the perfection of any collateral interest should be referred to bank counsel familiar with the state law in question.

The most troublesome perfection problems probably occur in the following two areas:

1. Personal property which either becomes affixed to real estate or which is part of some integrated process may be treated as a fixture under state law. Generally, a security interest in fixtures is perfected by filing on the real estate records in the county where the real estate is located, rather than a filing under the Uniform Commercial Code (UCC) in the county in the principal place of business of the debtor. Thus, if the personal property in question is a fixture, a failure to file in the real estate records results in a failure to perfect the security interest. On the other hand, if the personal property is held not to be a fixture, then a filing against the real estate records, without a UCC filing, would result in the security interest not being perfected. Obviously, the solution is to file in both places. Such a dual filing ensures that the collateral is perfected without regard to whether the personal property is held to be a fixture.

2. The second problem arises with certain types of collateral for which there are special filing requirements. Again, the bank must obtain the assistance of counsel and look to the law of that state in which the bank tries to enforce its collateral interest. Many states have special filing procedures for motor vehicles, motor homes, and the like. A failure to file under the right index might result in the loss by the bank of its security interest. As with fixtures, if the bank has any doubt about where a special item should be recorded, it should file both under the special filing procedures and under the general UCC personal property filing procedures.

A security interest is effective as between the bank and the debtor without any perfection. Perfecting the security interest protects the rights of the bank when parties other than the debtor come into the picture. These include other secured creditors, bona fide purchasers for value, and, most important, bankruptcy trustees. The bankruptcy trustee will seek to attack the perfection of the bank's security interest on any available ground. By invalidating the security interest of the bank, the trustee makes the security available to the unsecured creditors for whom he or she is representative.

Why Not Just Liquidate the Collateral?

If the bank has a $100,000 nonperforming loan and $200,000 of undoubted collateral value securing the loan, why should it not simply liquidate the collateral? There are several reasons for choosing some form of cooperative workout rather than collateral liquidation.

Relationship Considerations

If the customer provided more than sufficient collateral for the now-troubled loan, that may suggest there is something in the relationship worth preserving. It may suggest that the weakness in the loan results from the way the loan was originally structured. For example, the inability to reduce the level of outstanding indebtedness, which suggests a problem in the context of a term loan, may not in the context of some form of asset-based financing. The quick decision to eliminate the problem through collateral liquidation will generally sour the customer relationship. A genuine effort to rehabilitate the credit through restructure may preserve a relationship worth retaining. Even if the relationship is not one that the bank ultimately wants to retain, there may be public relations reasons for terminating the relationship on the most amicable basis possible. If some form of cooperative workout is inevitable, too hasty a move to liquidate collateral can make the atmosphere for the eventual workout more difficult.

Documentation Considerations

The bank may be aware of possible collateral deficiencies which it prefers not to reveal by a public testing of its collateral position through liquidation. If the bank's collateral contains some possibly fatal documentation weakness, it may be wise to move into some form of cooperative workout to correct the deficiencies and shore up the collateral with an eye toward future liquidation.

Litigation Considerations

The bank may reasonably anticipate that any effort to liquidate its collateral may provoke some litigation defense by the debtor. This can be of particular concern in specialized lending areas, such as agriculture where the local courts may be particularly protective of whole classes of debtors such as farmers. The debtor's initial litigation effort may be aimed at enjoining the bank's attempted foreclosure but may be coupled with a combination of those debtor defenses which we discuss in more depth in Chapter 8. The attempt to foreclose on the collateral may result in dragging the bank into protracted litigation on issues and in forums which the bank may prefer to avoid.

Bankruptcy Considerations

The effort to liquidate collateral may provoke a bankruptcy filing by the debtor which may result in extending, rather than shortening, the time to payout. A significant number of voluntary bankruptcy filings are precipitated by creditor moves to liquidate collateral.

Hidden Collateral Weaknesses

Banks are increasingly surprised to find that their collateral has some hidden liability that was not clear at the time the bank considered the liquidation question. Banks have been confronted with the postforeclosure surprise that their collateral has environmental, tax, or other obligations which diminish the value of the collateral taken, sometimes to the point of making the ownership of the collateral an absolute liability.

Nonearning Asset Considerations

Whereas a properly structured workout may permit the bank to continue to treat its loan as an earning asset, collateral liquidation may result in the bank's replacing the earning asset with a long-term, stagnant, nonearning asset. Few bankers are enchanted with the prospect of having a significant portion of their balance sheet comprised of other real estate owned.

Cost Considerations

The liquidation and holding of collateral entail hard costs. The most obvious costs are the legal costs required to liquidate. Less obvious costs include storage costs, disposition costs such as brokerage and auction fees, appraisal costs, insurance costs, and state real and personal property taxes. Hidden costs also include the bank's administrative and overhead costs associated with the holding and subsequent disposition of the foreclosed collateral.

Market Considerations

The bank must also consider whether it or the borrower can maximize the value of the collateral on disposition. In many cases, a cooperative borrower can dispose of collateral at higher prices than a bank can. The bank may be less familiar with the particular market and suffers from the obvious impediment of selling foreclosed property rather than selling in the ordinary course of business.

What About Other Creditors?

In considering whether to foreclose and how to foreclose on its collateral, the bank always should consider the position of other creditors. Often, the bank is only one of a number of creditors. In considering its strategy, it cannot overlook the impact of its actions on other creditors.

The "Herd" Factor

To say there is a herd instinct among creditors is not to be critical. Few persons and few banks have either the confidence or the recklessness to ignore what is going on around them. Collateral liquidation by one creditor inevitably creates concern or worse on the part of existing creditors. It generally makes it impossible for the debtor to convince new and potential creditors to put new money into the troubled enterprise. The bank that quickly opts for collateral liquidation should appreciate that its actions may pull the curtain down.

Involuntary Bankruptcy Possibility

The bank should carefully consider the degree to which the debtor has a sufficiently significant community of unsecured creditors to prompt their filing of an involuntary bankruptcy petition. Collateral liquidation by a major secured creditor is often the event that precipitates an involuntary filing.

Prior Secured Creditors

If the debtor has other secured creditors with prior security positions in some or all the collateral to be foreclosed on, the bank should carefully consider whether its postforeclosure position means servicing or paying off the secured indebtedness of other creditors before realizing on the collateral for its own debt. Similarly, the bank should consider if it is running risks and incurring expenses associated with collateral liquidation, only to remit some or all the proceeds from the sale of the collateral to some prior secured creditor.

Actions by Other Creditors

Even if the bank is fortunate to be both in a first position and to avoid an involuntary bankruptcy filing against the debtor, it may be the target of actions by subordinate secured or unsecured creditors, claiming that they were damaged by the bank's collateral liquidation. Many creditors have found themselves in postforeclosure litigation brought by other creditors having significant losses, a lot of anger, and little else to lose. They contend that they were damaged either by a foreclosure alleged to have been defective or by a disposition of the collateral in a manner resulting in either no return or inadequate return for other creditors. The fact that the target bank in such litigation may ultimately prevail does not eliminate the frustration, aggravation, and expense of such litigation.

Foreclosure

Once the bank has considered the benefits and risks of foreclosure and has determined to proceed, it confronts a new array of decisions, many of which involve judgments as to legal issues. Experienced legal counsel should be actively involved both in decisions concerning how to proceed and in the actual mechanics of the foreclosure.

Personal Property

• Cash. Probably the easiest form of collateral to liquidate and one to which the bank should quickly look is cash. Almost every form of note gives the bank a security interest in accounts and deposits maintained by the debtor with the bank. This security interest is perfected by the bank's possession of the accounts and generally can be liquidated simply by setoff.

A bank which has a loan in default and is considering whether and how to foreclose should monitor carefully the debtor's accounts to determine whether and when to setoff. Although it might be thought unusual for a debtor to simultaneously have a problem loan and significant cash deposits, it occurs often enough to put it on the consideration checklist. Accounts which may be set aside for specific purposes on the books or in the mind of the debtor, such as payroll accounts, corporate certificates of deposit, tax accounts, lockbox accounts, and the like, nevertheless may be available for setoff. The particular type of account may suggest more or less caution. But the bank certainly should consider what accounts it has and the extent to which it may be able to setoff against them.

• Marketable securities. Often a bank takes marketable securities as collateral. An initial concern is obviously whether collateral securities held are restricted. If so, the bank may confront the additional problems of complying with the requirements of Securities and Exchange Commission Rule 144 and finding purchasers who can meet the requirements of particular restrictions. The bank has possession of the original stock certificates and an assignment in blank. Foreclosure on such securities has a twofold advantage. First, it is generally a simple mechanical task of completing the assignment, a process which can be accomplished without either significant interaction with the debtor or publicity to other creditors. Second, the value of marketable securities can be readily determined at any point in time by reference to generally available price quotations.

It is a lot easier for a debtor or for other creditors to differ over the value of a piece of real estate than over 1,000 shares of stock listed on the New York Stock Exchange. Both these factors suggest that the bank, when fortunate enough to have such collateral, should closely monitor the market in the collateral securities as its loan moves into the problem category to determine whether and when to liquidate.

• Accounts receivable, inventory, and equipment. There is substantial uniformity among the laws of the various states concerning liquidation of accounts receivable, inventory, and equipment. This results from the adoption by most states of substantially similar versions of the UCC. Foreclosure is basically a two-step process involving getting possession of the collateral and disposing of the collateral.

Getting possession of the collateral can be obtained through:

1. Taking possession after default without judicial process if it can be done without "breach of the peace."
2. Voluntary surrender.
3. Judicial proceeding to obtain possession.

The preferred course is voluntary surrender. Voluntary surrender and cooperative disposition generally yield more dollars and entail less risk than the other possible courses. The bank can often persuade the debtor that it is in his or her best interest to so proceed.

The debtor's cooperation can make the critical difference in whether collateral disposition is successful. It does not matter whether the collateral involved is accounts receivable that need to be collected, inventory that needs to be sold in an orderly fashion, or equipment that can be best sold within the debtor's industry. Even the most "troubled" debtor is likely to know more about his or her accounts receivable and how to collect them, to know more about how to best dispose of inventory, and to know more about the potential purchasers for equipment than the banker.

Involving the debtor gives the process of collateral liquidation a much less disruptive appearance and makes it less likely that the bank will be sued over the manner in which it engaged in the process. Advance planning for the possibility of collateral liquidation either at the time the loan is made or early in the problem period can be particularly helpful. For example, a lockbox procedure for handling accounts receivable that has been in place for some time certainly facilitates the collection of accounts receivable. Similarly, obtaining lease assignments, landlord's waivers, and estoppel letters in advance can often facilitate the conduct of a quiet and gradual liquidation of inventory from the debtor's place of business. This makes it more likely that fair value will be obtained than a sale out of a truck or from some location remote from the debtor's regular place of business.

Obtaining possession of the collateral from the debtor is the first step. The second step is to determine the appropriate method of disposition. This is dictated by local law. Particular requirements must be noted and complied with, such as providing notice of the time and place of sale to the debtor and to other secured parties. Some states hold that guarantors are debtors for purposes of being entitled to notice of collateral disposition. Compliance with all technical requirements of local law is generally a prerequisite to obtaining a deficiency judgment for any balance that may be owing after collateral disposition.

Therefore, failure to comply with all technical aspects of local law can result in the bank's loss of deficiency rights. If the personal property collateral value represents only a small fraction of the debt owing, the bank may conclude to forego collateral disposition, rather than run the risk of losing deficiency rights. Alternatively, the bank might sue to obtain judgment for the entire amount of its indebtedness and then move against the collateral for application against the judgment obtained. This strategy minimizes the downside risks of technical defects in the disposition process.

The UCC in most states provides for two types of sale: public and private. Which course to follow can sometimes be a close and difficult question. The private sale permits greater flexibility in the sales process but is more likely to provoke questions as to whether the sale was "commercially reasonable." The public sale in most states is presumed to be commercially reasonable if the procedural requirements for such a sale are followed. The private sale may be accomplished with less attention and potentially adverse publicity.

The combination of greater flexibility and less publicity generally argues for the private sale. The element that most often argues for a public sale is the UCC prohibition against the secured party's buying at a private sale, except where the collateral is of a type customarily sold in a recognized market or is subject to widely distributed standard price quotations. Where the collateral is not of such a type, the secured party may want to hold a public sale, buy the property, and resell the collateral for its own account.

Real Property

There is substantial variance from state to state with regard to real property foreclosures. Some states require the bringing of a civil action; some states require judicial sales. Other states permit private sales conducted by the secured party under various forms of powers of attorney. Some states have lengthy redemption periods for the benefit of the debtor; other states do not. Some states require court confirmation of real property foreclosure sales prices as a prerequisite to any deficiency judgment; others do not.

The banker must be particularly sensitive to working with legal counsel to ensure that the mechanics of local law are followed precisely. Indeed, even when legal counsel is actively involved, the possible pitfalls are such that careful counsel may advise suit to obtain judgment on the note prior to foreclosure to protect the bank's deficiency rights. Obtaining judgment for the entire amount of its debt frees the bank to proceed with foreclosure with less concern about the loss of its deficiency rights.

Summary

Collateral liquidation is often the quickest way for the bank to obtain payout, but it must be approached with care. A false step can be costly. As the relationships between bankers and lawyers become more transaction-oriented, the possibility of such a false step can increase. The banker may tell the lawyer to foreclose on one piece of real estate collateral. If the lawyer is not aware that there are other pieces of real estate collateral and several guarantors, he or she may accomplish the requested foreclosure but unwittingly put the bank's deficiency rights in jeopardy by not properly planning for moving against other collateral or not notifying the guarantors of the sale. Collateral liquidation should be approached on a strategic basis that looks at the entire collateral package and determines an overall liquidation plan.

Reducing the Debt to Judgment 8

The time comes in the life of some problem credits when the lender determines to convert its debt into a judgment. Like the note itself, a judgment is a piece of paper. What is it about the piece of paper called a judgment that makes it superior to the piece of paper called a note?

A judgment evidences a court decision that settles the respective rights and claims of the lender and borrower. Since the judgment is a court decision both on the facts and the law, it precludes not only redetermination of the facts and the law considered by the court in awarding the judgment but also precludes a later assertion of defenses or counterclaims which might have been asserted in the action giving rise to the judgment, but for whatever reason were not asserted. Thus, obtaining a judgment ought to put to rest once and for all the borrower's defensive or counterclaim issues. The judgment is also conclusive on the lender on such issues as the principal amount outstanding and the interest owing through the date of judgment. If, for example, the lender failed to include a default rate of interest in its judgment, the lender is nevertheless bound by the interest rate stated in the judgment. From the judgment date forward, interest accrues on the judgment at whatever rate is provided for by the law of the state giving the judgment.

The judgment, in addition to precluding the borrower's later assertion of defenses and counterclaims, also is superior to the note in giving the lender an arsenal of collection weapons not available to one who simply holds a note. This arsenal, discussed in Chapter 9 "Collecting the Judgment," includes the lien rights obtained when the lender records the judgment, the right to engage in postjudgment discovery to find the borrower's assets, the rights of levy and attachment, the right of garnishment, and perhaps other remedies provided for judgment creditors by state law. In addition, obtaining judgment enhances the lender's ability to obtain appointment of a receiver and to set aside conveyances of property made by the borrower for inadequate consideration. Obtaining this arsenal may prompt the lender's decision to reduce the debt to judgment.

Deciding to reduce debt to judgment and the time and expense entailed in doing so vary depending on the defenses and counterclaims which the borrower is likely to assert. These defenses and counterclaims vary according to state law and the inventiveness and aggressiveness of borrower's counsel. There are, however, a growing number of potential borrower issues which the lender may have to hurdle to obtain judgment. These borrower issues are listed, with an example and a brief analysis of the issue, in the following pages.

Fraud in the Inducement

Example

The borrower claims to have signed a note, a guarantee, a security agreement, a mortgage, or some other document but did not know what he was signing. He was told that it was just the lender's standard form. He was not told that the note signed granted the lender a security interest in all his bank accounts. He was not told that the security agreement he signed covering all his company's inventory and accounts receivable secured not only a small single purpose loan to purchase a new computer but also secured all other indebtedness, however and whenever incurred, even where the other indebtedness previously had been unsecured.

Comment

This is a difficult issue for the borrower. It is the law in most states that one who has the capacity to read and who signs a written contract is bound by the contract unless execution was obtained by some sort of trick. The lender is, therefore, likely to prevail unless the note was signed by a borrower unable to read, unless the borrower was prevented by the lender from reading what was signed, or unless the borrower was affirmatively misled by the lender. This issue can be blunted if the lender deals with reasonably sophisticated borrowers and encourages them to read what they sign and to obtain the assistance of counsel prior to signing loan documents.

Waiver

Example

The borrower contends that although its note provides for a $100,000 balloon payment at the end of 24 months, the lender nevertheless gave assurance that the $100,000 would then be put on a five-year installment loan. The borrower, therefore, contends that the lender has waived its right to insist upon the full $100,000 balloon payment specified in the note.

Comment

If the conversation took place, then whether the lender waived its right to insist on the full $100,000 balloon payment may turn on when the conversation took place. If it took place before the borrower signed the note, then the lender is probably protected by legal doctrines such as the parol evidence rule, integration, and merger. These doctrines provide that prior inconsistent statements are controlled by subsequent written agreements. If the conversation is alleged to have taken place after the signing of the original note and is supported by consideration, the lender may well have waived its right to judgment for the full amount of the $100,000 balloon. Oral understandings with the borrower inconsistent with the terms of written contracts between the lender and the borrower should be avoided.

Waiver of Strict Performance

Example

The note signed by the borrower provides that if any installment payments are not made when due, the entire indebtedness can be accelerated and the security interests given foreclosed. The borrower has regularly been between 10 and 35 days late with every installment payment for 16 months, without the lender having accelerated or foreclosed. Finally, the lender, having had enough, accelerates the note and tries to foreclose. The borrower argues that there has been a mutual departure from the terms of the original contract and that the lender has waived its right to strict performance.

Comment

Under the law of many jurisdictions, the borrower would have a strong argument. If the lender wants to return the relationship to one of strict performance, it should notify the borrower of its intention to enforce the contract strictly in the future. If late payments are thereafter accepted, then the lender might require a written acknowledgment from the borrower that the lender in accepting the late payment was not waiving any right to insist on strict compliance with loan documents.

Failure of Consideration

Example

The borrower has a $100,000 unsecured loan and determines that it may need a seasonal line of an additional $100,000. The lender agrees to the additional $100,000 line but insists on obtaining a security interest covering the borrower's accounts receivable and inventory to secure it. The security agreement given has "open-end" or "dragnet" language, that is, the security interest given is to secure "any and all indebtedness." The $100,000 additional line never gets funded, but the lender later seeks to foreclose on the security interest in the accounts receivable and inventory as a result of the borrower's default on the original $100,000 unsecured loan. The borrower contends that there was no consideration for its giving of the security interest in the inventory and accounts receivable, since the original $100,000 loan had been made on an unsecured basis and since the additional $100,000 line was never funded.

Comment

Whether there was a failure of consideration in the lender's obtaining the collateral may turn on why the $100,000 line was never funded. If the lender refused to fund the line after requested to do so, then there probably was a failure of consideration and the lender should not be able to foreclose on the security interest in the accounts receivable and inventory to satisfy the $100,000 loan which was originally unsecured. If, however, the line was available, but the borrower for whatever reason failed to draw on it, then that availability is consideration supporting the grant of the security interest in the accounts receivable and inventory.

Material Alteration

Example

The borrower signed a note in blank. The bank later filled in the amount and the date. Later, the loan goes into default, and the lender sues. The borrower defends on the ground that the note was materially altered and that the borrower was not even in the country on the date that the note was purportedly signed.

Comment

The Uniform Commercial Code (UCC) provides that the negotiability of an instrument is unaffected by the fact that it is undated, antedated, or postdated (UCC §3–114). The code also provides that when an instrument has been completed in accordance with authority given the lender, then the instrument is effective (UCC §3–115). The UCC further provides that the burden of establishing any unauthorized completion is on the party asserting unauthorized completion (UCC §3–115). Thus, unless the borrower can show that the note sued on has been completed in a manner inconsistent with the original understanding as between lender and borrower, then the lender should prevail. Generally, it should be a relatively simple matter to trace the dollars as reflected on the completed note and the disbursement of loan proceeds.

Joint Venture

Example

The lender has a tract of "other real estate" which it obtained in foreclosure. It sells the property to the borrower, financing the land acquisition and committing a construction loan for development of a shopping center. The borrower gives the bank a note and a mortgage. The note goes into default and, after foreclosing on the property, the lender sues the borrower for a deficiency judgment. The borrower contends that the relationship with the lender was never a debtor-creditor relationship but rather a joint venture relationship, with the borrower contributing management and development expertise and the lender contributing money. The borrower argues that since the joint venture failed, both the lender and the borrower lose. The borrower cannot get back its time and expertise and the lender cannot get back its money.

Comment

This is a difficult issue for the borrower. The lender should be able to prevail unless there was some written partnership agreement between the lender and the borrower, unless the lender was entitled to some share of the profits from the development enterprise, unless the interest rate was somehow keyed to the success of the project, or unless the lender has some ownership interest in or control over the property other than just its mortgage interest.

Securities Fraud

Example

The borrower and his banker have lunch and discuss potential investments. The borrower then takes out a loan with the bank, the proceeds of which are used to make one of the investments which had been discussed. The investment later goes sour, and the loan goes into default. The lender sues, and the borrower defends on the ground that the entire transaction was one "investment contract," in which the bank violated various anti-fraud provisions of the federal or state securities laws.

Comment

This is a difficult issue for the borrower. If the lender did not sell the borrower anything other than the use of money, then the lender should not have any liability under state or federal securities laws. Extending credit is not selling a security and in and of itself should not give rise to any violation of securities laws.

Failure to Preserve Collateral

Example

The lender has a secured loan to the borrower. On the loan's default, the lender forecloses on the collateral but obtains a price for the collateral substantially less than what the borrower thinks it is worth. When sued for the loan's deficiency balance, the borrower asserts that the lender failed to preserve the collateral, resulting in the borrower's discharge.

Comment

The UCC provides that the holder of a note discharges any party to the note to the extent that *without such party's consent* the holder unjustifiably impairs collateral (UCC §3–606). Most lenders have note and security agreement forms that contain the broadest possible provisions empowering the bank to take control of and exercise rights in collateral. The case law in most states holds such language sufficient to constitute the consent referred to in UCC §3–606.

Failure to Comply with UCC in Collateral Disposition

Example

The lender has a secured loan to the borrower. On default, the lender disposes of the collateral and sues the borrower for the deficiency balance on the loan. The borrower contends that the disposition of the collateral was not in compliance with UCC §9–504, in not being either commercially reasonable or procedurally correct. The borrower contends that this bars the lender's right to a deficiency judgment.

Comment

The law in many states requires strict compliance with all the requirements of UCC §9–504 as a condition precedent to recovery of any deficiency judgment against the borrower. Some states also hold that a guarantor is a borrower for the purposes of the requirements of UCC §9–504 and that language in a guarantee purporting to waive rights conferred by §9–504 is ineffective under UCC §9–501. Thus, if the borrower or a guarantor can show that there was not strict compliance with UCC §9–504, then they may be able to successfully defend against deficiency actions against them.

Failure to Fund

Example

The lender makes a construction loan to the borrower. When the loan comes due, the borrower is unable to pay. When sued, the borrower defends on the ground that the lender agreed to make a permanent loan on the project and that the failure of the lender to fund the permanent loan provides a defense to the lender's suit on the construction loan.

Comment

The law in most states is that a lender's refusal to make a second loan, even after a representation that it might make a second loan, does not bar the lender from recovery of the amount owed under the first loan. This does not necessarily preclude the debtor from suing the lender for breach of the second loan commitment. But in order for a promise to lend money to be enforceable, most states require agreement between the potential lender and borrower on the amount of the loan, the rate of interest, the term, and other necessary elements. This burden is often more than the borrower can carry.

Creditor Domination

Example

The lender has a loan agreement with the borrower which places tight financial controls on the borrower, even to restricting the borrower's ability to make management changes not approved by the lender. The borrower is losing money and proposes to make certain management changes which the lender refuses to approve. The borrower continues to lose money and ultimately cannot repay its debt to the lender. When sued, the borrower defends and counterclaims, contending that the lender's unreasonable domination of its affairs caused its inability to repay its loans. In addition, this resulted in substantial losses for which the lender is responsible.

Comment

This is a recent borrower defense that has met with dramatic success in at least one case. The law in this area is still in a formative stage. The lender response should be tied to its good faith exercise of specific rights conferred on it by contract with the borrower.

Failure to Exercise Creditor Rights in Good Faith

Example

The lender has a demand loan to the borrower. The loan agreement provides that the lender can cease funding in its discretion at any time and without notice to the borrower and can demand payment of any amount already outstanding. The lender determines that the borrower's financial condition is deteriorating and ceases making additional advances. This results in the borrower's checks to its suppliers being returned and the eventual liquidation of the borrower. The lender sues for the amount of its loans. The borrower defends and counterclaims based on the failure of the lender to exercise its rights in good faith.

Comment

This is another emerging borrower issue in which the law is in a formative stage. The argument is based on UCC §1–203 which provides: "Every contract or duty within this title imposes an obligation of good faith on its performance or enforcement." At least some courts have held that where a lender has clear rights under its loan documents, they must nevertheless be exercised in good faith. If the borrower can produce some facts which throw into question the good faith of the lender's exercise of its rights, then a jury question may be presented. In at least one case, this argument resulted in a sizable jury verdict against a major bank.

Tying

Example

The lender makes a capital loan to an automobile dealership conditioned on the dealer's selling a substantial share of its retail paper to the lender and employing a person designated by the lender to review and sell to the lender approved retail paper. The loan goes into default, and the lender sues the dealer. The dealer defends and counterclaims, stating that the requirement that the dealer sell the lender retail paper is an unlawful tying of one product to another, entitling the dealer to treble damages.

Comment

The Federal Bank Holding Company Act amendments of 1970 added an "anti-tying" provision (12 U.S.C. §1972 and §1975). This statute says that a bank shall not extend credit or sell property or services and tie the sale of the credit or service to the customer's having to obtain some other credit or service from the bank or some company affiliated with the bank, except where the condition or requirement imposed by the bank is one that the bank "shall reasonably impose in a credit transaction to insure the soundness of the credit". The law provides that any person injured by any violation of the statute may sue in federal court and recover three times the actual damages sustained, plus attorneys' fees. There has been little litigation interpreting this law. But in a period of increasing product deregulation and resulting proliferation and creative packaging of bank services, this is likely to be a defense increasingly asserted by borrowers. The ultimate test is probably whether the lender required the borrower to do something not traditionally related to, or usually provided for in, the simple making of a loan. In many cases, this will be a jury question.

Prime Rate

Example

The lender extends a loan to the borrower at an interest rate tied to the lender's prime, "best," "base," or some other announced rate. The loan goes into default. The lender sues the borrower who defends and counterclaims that it was charged a rate purportedly tied to the best rate available from the lender. But, in fact, the lender had other loans to other customers at rates lower than the announced rate to which the borrower's interest rate was tied. The borrower contends that this is a breach of contract and constitutes fraud. This borrower issue is sometimes coupled with a issue relating to the computation of interest on either a 360- or 365-day base, which may result in a yield fractionally in excess of the stated rate.

Comment

This is a new borrower issue which has seen increasing recent use. While there is little authority adverse to lenders, the potential for substantial damage awards has prompted some prime rate cases to be settled at very large dollar amounts.

RICO

Example

The lender has committed some arguable contract breach such as failure to fund, creditor domination, failure to exercise rights in good faith, charging a rate in excess of that contracted for, or the like. The loan goes into default. The lender sues the borrower, and the borrower defends and counterclaims alleging the specific breach. But the borrower adds an allegation that the breach was committed by use of the mails and telephone so as to constitute mail fraud, wire fraud, bankruptcy fraud, theft by deception, or some other crime. All of this is alleged to constitute a violation of the federal Racketeer Influenced and Corrupt Organizations Act (RICO), entitling the borrower to treble damages.

Comment

This is another emerging borrower issue. RICO refers to 18 U.S.C. §1961 et. seq. and similar legislation enacted by a number of states modelled after the federal law. RICO defines a "pattern of racketeering activity" which includes two specified criminal acts within a ten-year period. Once a pattern of racketeering activity has been alleged, the statute makes it illegal for one to invest income derived from the "pattern" to acquire or operate any enterprise engaged in interstate commerce or to maintain an interest in or control of an enterprise engaged in interstate commerce through the "pattern." If the borrower alleges it has been injured in its business or property by reason of activity unlawful under RICO, then the borrower is permitted to ask for three times its actual damages, plus attorneys' fees. Although there have been increasing numbers of RICO claims lodged against lenders in recent years, there has been little actual recovery. Nevertheless, this is an increasingly troubling borrower issue.

Summary

This list of borrower issues is not intended to be exclusive. Obviously, there are such basic defenses as the borrower's never having signed the note which are not covered. Also, the inventiveness of aggressive borrower counsel will continually add issues to the list. However, the list does present a number of arguments available to frustrate, to delay, and to make more expensive the lender's effort to reduce its debt to judgment.

Lenders can long wistfully for the halcyon days when the rights of creditors were favored by the law. The Georgia Supreme Court in 1878 stated: "The true law, everywhere and at all times, delighteth in the payment of just debts. Blessed is the man that pays. The practice of paying promptly, and to the last cent, tends to the cultivation of one of the most excellent traits of human character. If debtors were guided by their own true interest, on an enlarged scale, they would be even more clamorous to pay than creditors are to receive. Tender would be more frequent than calls for money. Debt is the source of much unhappiness. The best possible thing to be done with a debt is to pay it" (*Robert v. N.&A.F. Tift*, 60 Ga. 566, 571 [1878]). Unfortunately for today's lenders, longing for such a bygone era will not bring it back. Today, reducing debt to judgment can be a long, arduous, and expensive process.

The absolute optimum timetable for reducing debt to final judgment in most states is too long. A suit on a note filed in early January would be answered in early February. Assuming no serious borrower defenses, the lender can file a motion for summary judgment which, even if filed in early February, would rarely be disposed of until sometime in March. If the lender is successful in obtaining summary judgment on all issues, the borrower's notice of appeal would be filed in April and the record transmitted and the case docketed in the appellate court in May or June. All briefs in the appellate court probably would not be filed until August. Oral argument might be held in September or October, and, in most states, it would be the fortunate lender indeed that had obtained a final judgment within the year in which the suit was initiated.

If the borrower's counsel is able to create any fact issue at all on any of the borrower issues, then the process of obtaining the final judgment may well stretch out for years. All the while, the borrower's assets are subject to dissipation, and the borrower's financial condition subject to deterioration. The lender is receiving neither principal nor interest but is receiving the continuing aggravation of complying with litigation discovery that saps energy, spirit, and time. The lender also faces legal bills that may mount up into tens and hundreds of thousands of dollars.

Many a lender who has won each and every litigation battle concludes that the war was lost. By the time the litigation was finally concluded, the goal of collecting the debt may have slipped over the horizon. Finding lenders who can fondly recall their litigation experiences is rare and unfortunately becoming even more so.

Able and experienced lender counsel can minimize the damage and delay that the lender may confront in reducing its debt to judgment and can minimize the sense of frustration and desperation that all too often sets in during the litigation. A continuing dialogue between the lender and counsel is necessary to ensure that both realize that the litigation is not an end in itself, but merely a tool to the end of collecting the debt.

Collecting the Judgment 9

Chapter 8 addressed some of the reasons why the bank might decide to try to obtain a judgment. This chapter expands on some of the weapons which the judgment makes available to the bank.

Postjudgment Discovery

One frustration during the attempt to reduce the debt to judgment is the inability to obtain accurate financial information on the debtor and the debtor's assets. One often has the uneasy feeling that the litigation is used for delay while the assets of the debtor are being hidden, transferred, or otherwise removed from the bank's reach. Often this fear is well founded.

Interrogatories

Once the bank obtains judgment, then the availability of postjudgment discovery allows the bank to investigate the debtor's financial affairs. The first step usually is a well-drafted set of postjudgment interrogatories. These interrogatories should inquire into the sources of income available to the debtor; monies owed to the debtor; automobiles, boats, planes, and other major personal property items either owned by or at the disposal of the debtor; inventories of personal property including art work, antiques, expensive jewelry, and other household and personal goods; information concerning banking, savings, and other deposit accounts; real estate owned; partnership interests, stocks, bonds, mortgages, and other securities; life insurance policies, legacies, and other expectancy interests; and whatever other financial information the bank and its attorneys may think useful.

Depositions

Postjudgment interrogatories are usually followed by postjudgment depositions of the debtor and other parties likely to have knowledge of the debtor's assets and financial affairs. If the bank was able to get answers to its postjudgment interrogatories, they should provide the roadmap for the conduct of the postjudgment deposition. Gaps in the answers can be filled in and additional information sought. The answers to the interrogatories and the debtor's deposition may also suggest other persons who know about the debtor's assets and finances. These persons may be likely subjects for postjudgment interrogatories or depositions; they include financial advisors, accountants, stockbrokers, other creditors, business associates, and family members.

Postjudgment discovery is often met with resistance. The debtor may refuse to answer interrogatories and may refuse to appear at scheduled depositions. He or she may appear but object to testifying about particular subjects. The objections may extend from refusals to testify on the grounds that the testimony may work a forfeiture of the debtor's estate to refusals based on the Fifth Amendment privilege against self-incrimination. The judgment creditor must simply anticipate resistance and gird for the battle.

The judgment creditor should quickly and forcefully bring to the attention of the appropriate court that the judgment rights obtained by the creditor after long and expensive litigation are now being intentionally frustrated by the debtor. The creditor must not only ask for court orders compelling the postjudgment discovery but should also insist that the court award expenses incurred in having to force the debtor to comply with the discovery. On occasion, creditors have had to take postjudgment discovery before a judge to impress the debtor with the seriousness of their intention to obtain the information to which they were entitled.

The ultimate purpose of postjudgment discovery is to find assets of the debtor. Once assets are found, the focus shifts to how to get them.

Levy

Levy is the seizure of property by an officer authorized by local law to take and hold property until it can be sold and the proceeds applied to payment of the creditor's judgment. In some jurisdictions, the levying officer is the sheriff, in others, the marshal. When the judgment creditor uncovers some item of property belonging to the debtor, the creditor directs the levying officer to it and instructs the officer to levy upon and sell a sufficient portion of it to satisfy the judgment.

Levying on the Property

The levying officer either performs an actual levy or, if the property is too large, bulky, or unmanageable for an actual levy, a constructive levy. The levying officer often is reluctant to seize property and expects the judgment creditor to specify those items which are to be subjected to the levy. The debtor often contends that items subjected to levy belonged to someone else or were held on consignment. If the debtor can prove the truth of such contentions, the judgment creditor and the levying officer can find themselves defendants in litigation alleging a wrongful levy.

Public Sale

Once the debtor's property has been subjected to levy, either actual or constructive, the property is prepared for public sale. This may involve storing the property while it is advertised for judicial sale. It may simply involve tagging property that has been subjected to constructive levy and advertising it for sale where it is located. The procedures for the conduct of judicial sales are spelled out by state law which may designate the date of sale, the place of sale, the hours of sale, and the manner of advertising for the sale. The actual sale is an auction where the property is exposed for bidding by the officer authorized to conduct such sales.

Potential bidders may include both the judgment creditor and the judgment debtor. If the judgment creditor is concerned that the bids on particular items are below their value, he may bid in the items and either hold them or resell them for his own account. The judgment creditor bids with credits against the judgment, rather than cash. On occasion, the judgment debtor attends the sale to buy back his own property. If the judgment debtor is the successful bidder, the creditor may subject the property to a second levy and try to sell it again.

Sales proceeds are generally distributed first to the expenses of the sale, then to the holders of any prior security interests or liens, and then to payment of the judgment creditor for whose benefit the sale was conducted. Any remaining excess would then be paid to subordinate lien creditors and then the debtor. In some states, there can be no levy and sale on real property if there are outstanding mortgage or security deed holders. In such case, the judgment creditor may have to pay off the holder of any prior secured debt in order to subject the real estate to judicial sale.

The judgment creditor should determine what exemptions from levy and sale are provided by local law. There are significant variations from state to state, and states provide for varying homestead exemptions. Some states provide exemptions for support obligations for widows. There are varying treatments for execution sales on jointly owned property. The judgment creditor should be attentive to the specific requirements and exemptions of the law of the jurisdiction where the execution is to be conducted.

Garnishment

Garnishment is a remedy that varies from state to state but generally permits a creditor to hold or seize money or other property of the judgment debtor in the hands of some third party. The most usual examples involve garnishment of wages held by an employer to be paid to the employee debtor, and monies held by a bank which belong to the judgment debtor. State law determines the extent of the garnishment remedy. Both state and federal law set limitations on the amount of a debtor's wages which can be subject to garnishment. Pensions are often exempt from garnishment, and special rules are often established for child support and alimony obligations.

The effectiveness of this technique is often measured more in getting the debtor's attention and disrupting the debtor's affairs than in actually capturing large sums of money. Sometimes levy and garnishment may push the debtor to the point of a voluntary bankruptcy filing.

Receivership

A receivership is a proceeding brought by creditors when property of the debtor is in danger of destruction, loss, or other material injury or where the property is subject to rapid diminution in value because there is no one to manage it. It is an equitable proceeding, the primary purpose of which is to take charge of, manage, and preserve the debtor's property.

It is rarely used by judgment creditors for several reasons:

1. Receiver's primary purpose is to manage and preserve the property not to liquidate it for the benefit of the creditors.

2. Receiver acts for creditors generally not just the particular judgment creditor that may have filed the receivership petition.

3. Receiver becomes an intervening party standing between the debtor and the judgment creditor and may actually protect the debtor from the judgment creditor.

4. Fee schedules set by state law for paying receivers often cause the receivership proceeding to be an expensive way to try to collect a debt.

Setting Aside Fraudulent Conveyances

Few things are as frustrating to the judgment creditor as finally obtaining a judgment, only to find that the debtor has used the litigation period to transfer the assets to protect them from the judgment ultimately obtained. Conveyances made to defraud creditors may be set aside. The procedure for doing so and the definition of what constitutes a fraudulent conveyance are matters of local law. Generally, however, three types of conveyance are subject to being set aside:

1. Transfers by insolvent debtors to third parties where the debtor reserves some rights in the property after assignment.

2. Transfers which are intended to delay or defraud creditors and where the transferee is aware of the transferor's intent.

3. Transfers by insolvent debtors not for valuable consideration.

Actions to set aside fraudulent conveyances are difficult, and proving that the debtor is insolvent can be difficult. Proving that a particular transfer was intended to defraud a creditor and that the transferee was aware of that intent requires proof of what is in the mind of two different and often related parties. Moreover, neither of the parties is subject to the control of the judgment creditor nor sympathetic to his interests.

Judgment Collection by Agreement

The tools available to one holding a judgment, generally called the judgment creditor, are limited. If the judgment creditor is to be successful in collecting the debt in full, he or she must make imaginative use of these limited tools. Some items of personal property can be subjected to levy and converted into cash fairly quickly and easily. These include marketable securities, vehicles, and perhaps certain items of expensive equipment. Trying to collect a large commercial judgment by levying on file cabinets and water coolers can be a tiresome and unproductive exercise. On the other hand, most businesses have certain personal property for which there may be little or no market, but its seizure may have an extremely disruptive impact on the debtor's operations. Such items range from computers and computer tapes to key components on an assembly line.

The purpose of the levy becomes not so much to convert assets into cash as to maximize the disruption of the debtor's business. Other items of personal property may have minimal dollar value but very high symbolic value. Attaching the chief executive officer's furniture may not yield maximum dollars but may ensure that your judgment gets high level attention. Similarly, garnishments that may not result in the capture of accounts with significant dollar balances may, nevertheless, have a significantly disruptive and embarrassing effect on the debtor's business. The debtor's cash flow may be totally disrupted and the embarrassment significant.

While an action to set aside a fraudulent conveyance to a wife may not ultimately result in return of the property, it may be the first time that the debtor's wife has had to come face to face with the possibility of depositions, adverse lawyers, court appearances, and the like. Many a debtor becomes more amenable to paying the judgments once a spouse, relatives, and friends have been brought into the vortex of the debt.

The remedies provided to a judgment creditor are not always sufficient to result in payoff. They can, however, be combined in an aggressive assault which may result in the debtor's voluntary agreement to pay. Such an agreement typically takes the form of an Agreement to Refrain from Execution which stays in place only as long as the judgment debtor performs in repaying the debt as agreed. On default, the debtor would once again be subject to the next barrage of postjudgment collection activities.

Fundamental Concepts of Bankruptcy 10

Usually, bankruptcy does not come as a surprise to the bank officer. The sophisticated borrower has bankruptcy counsel and uses the threat of bankruptcy as part of negotiations with the bank. A grounding in basic bankruptcy law and procedure assists the bank officer in evaluating the strength of the borrower's negotiating position and also improves communication between the banker and legal counsel.

Overview of the Bankruptcy Law

We will treat only bankruptcies under Chapter 7 or Chapter 11. Chapter 7 bankruptcies are liquidation cases, where a trustee is put in place to collect and liquidate the debtor's assets and pay creditors in accordance with the rules of distribution set forth in the Bankruptcy Code. Chapter 11 cases are those in which the debtor hopes to reorganize its business under the protection of the bankruptcy court. Ordinarily, the debtor stays in possession of its property and proposes a plan of reorganization which is voted on by the creditors. In some Chapter 11 cases, particularly in a case where there is fraud or gross mismanagement on the part of the debtor's present management, a trustee may be appointed to manage the debtor's business. Chapter 11 cases can be converted to Chapter 7 cases, and vice versa.

Chapter 13 bankruptcy—cases limited to the adjustment of debts of individuals with regular income—is not discussed in this book because commercial borrowers are less likely to file a Chapter 13 case, as compared with a Chapter 11 case.

The Bankruptcy Code is comprised of not only Chapter 7, 11, and 13 but also Chapters 1, 3, 5, and 9. Chapter 9 relates only to the adjustment of debts of a municipality and is not dealt with here. Chapters 1, 3, and 5 contain the ground rules of bankruptcy, and the provisions of those chapters are applicable to cases arising under either Chapter 7 or Chapter 11.

Automatic Stay

The automatic stay is probably the best known feature of the bankruptcy laws. On the filing of either a voluntary or an involuntary petition in bankruptcy, the automatic stay comes into effect.

Scope

The automatic stay stops the bank from taking virtually any action against the debtor, property of the debter, or property of the bankruptcy estate. To be more specific, the bank cannot:

- Commence or continue any lawsuit against the debtor that was (or could have been) commenced before the beginning of the bankruptcy case.
- Commence or continue any lawsuit against the debtor to recover a claim against the debtor that arose before the commencement of the case.
- Enforce against the debtor or against property of the estate a judgment obtained before the commencement of the case.
- Take any act to obtain possession of property of the estate or property from the estate or to exercise control over property of the estate.
- Take any act to create, perfect, or enforce any lien against property of the estate.
- Take any act to create, perfect, or enforce against property of the debtor any lien to the extent that such lien secures a claim that arose before the commencement of the case.
- Take any act to collect, assess, or recover a claim against the debtor that arose before the commencement of the case.
- Setoff any debt owing to the debtor that arose before the commencement of the case against any claim against the debtor.

Obviously, every traditional collection method or device to which a lender would ordinarily turn (or may have turned to prior to the filing of the bankruptcy case) is stopped dead in its tracks by the automatic stay. The automatic stay is designed to prevent the "dismemberment" of a debtor, and the bankruptcy courts take violations of the automatic stay quite seriously, as we discuss later on in this chapter.

For a banker, one of the more significant prohibitions of the automatic stay is the prohibition against setoffs. If the automatic stay means what it says, what is to prevent the debtor from withdrawing funds on deposit and defeating the right of setoff? Fortunately, although there is some case authority to the contrary, most courts have held that a bank is entitled to freeze any funds to which there is a bona fide right of setoff.

Some courts require a bank, immediately on performing a freeze, to file appropriate papers with the bankruptcy court to get the court's permission for the freeze. Accordingly, where a debtor files bankruptcy and the bank has a right to setoff, counsel should be immediately contacted so that an appropriate strategy, consistent with the governing case law of the appropriate district, may be implemented.

Another important area is garnishments. If the bank is trying to collect a judgment by garnishing a third party that owes money to the bank's debtor, when bankruptcy intervenes the bank has an *affirmative* duty to dismiss the garnishment proceeding. Failure to dismiss such a garnishment will be a violation of the automatic stay. Therefore, when the banker learns of the borrower's bankruptcy he or she should immediately notify any lawyer who has been trying to collect the debt.

One of the more important things to understand about the automatic stay is that it applies only to the debtor. Actions against third parties not in bankruptcy, such as guarantors or partners liable for partnership debts, may continue unless a specific court order to the contrary is obtained.

Exceptions

There are 11 exceptions to the automatic stay. For example, a debtor cannot avoid the continuation of criminal proceedings against it merely by filing a bankruptcy petition. None of these exceptions is of any particular importance to bankers with respect to the banker's ordinary collection efforts. However, one or more of these exceptions could have a significant impact on the debtor's ability to maintain its business, and that impact would, of course, have a bearing on the banker's evaluation of the viability of the debtor's business. For example, in certain instances, governmental units are not prohibited from commencing or continuing proceedings which are within their police or regulatory power. Thus, it is arguable that an enforcement proceeding by the Securities and Exchange Commission might be commenced or continued notwithstanding bankruptcy.

When Is the Automatic Stay Effective?

As noted, the automatic stay comes into effect on the filing of a bankruptcy petition. Ordinarily, a banker may vigorously pursue collection efforts until he or she actually learns of the filing of a bankruptcy case. However, at least one bankruptcy court has placed a *duty to inquire* on creditors if they have reason to believe that a bankruptcy petition by the debtor is imminent. Accordingly, it might be wise to inquire whether or not a petition has actually been filed before taking particular affirmative collection steps if the debtor, or his counsel, has stated to the banker that a bankruptcy case is in the process of being filed. Typically, however, if a foreclosure (or similar action) is scheduled for a particular time, the debtor's counsel will file the bankruptcy petition prior to the scheduled foreclosure and will contact the bank or the bank's counsel to inform them that the automatic stay has gone into effect.

Sanctions for Violation of the Automatic Stay

Violations of the automatic stay are not taken lightly by bankruptcy judges. Courts have awarded compensatory damages, costs, and attorneys' fees to the debtor, and, in "appropriate" cases, punitive damages have been assessed. A recent amendment to the bankruptcy law provides that an individual injured by any willful violation of the automatic stay *shall* recover actual damages, including costs and attorneys' fees, and, in appropriate circumstances, may recover punitive damages. In addition to these sanctions, the bank may find its claim subordinated to the claims of all other creditors. Obviously, the prohibitions of the automatic stay must be taken seriously, and the grave consequences for violating the automatic stay should not be forgotten.

Actions in Violation of the Automatic Stay Are Void

If the bank has inadvertently (or otherwise) violated the automatic stay, the "advantage" it gained, such as having repossessed collateral, may be undone by the bankruptcy court. The courts have ruled that an action taken in violation of the automatic stay—even where the action was taken in ignorance that the bankruptcy case had been filed—is void. For example, a foreclosure sale conducted in violation of the stay will leave the purchaser without good title.

Concept of a Claim

While the banker usually thinks in terms of a customer's debt to the bank, the Bankruptcy Code speaks in terms of the bank's "claim." Where the bank has only an unsecured debt, the bank's claim includes the principal amount owed by the debtor, with interest accrued as of the date of the filing of the bankruptcy petition. The general rule in bankruptcy is that interest stops accruing on unsecured claims on the filing of the bankruptcy case. The unsecured claim may also include prepetition late charges, attorneys' fees which came due prepetition by virtue of the provisions of the note, and other costs or charges that are part of the customer's liability to the bank under the note.

If the bank is fully secured, its claim can include postpetition interest in addition to the prepetition interest up to the value of its collateral. If the promissory note includes an agreement by the debtor to pay the attorneys' fees of the bank, then even if state law would not permit the enforcement of such a claim, the Bankruptcy Code allows the oversecured creditor to collect reasonable attorneys' fees, up to the value of its collateral.

At what rate does postpetition interest accrue? The answer to this question is not settled. Some bankruptcy courts hold that postpetition interest is not necessarily calculated at the interest rate provided by the agreement. Instead, these cases say that "equitable" principles govern. One bankruptcy court has suggested that the allowance of postpetition interest is analogous to interest on a judgment, which accrues at the rate allowed by law—not at the contractual rate applicable to the indebtedness for which the judgment was obtained. Many courts have ruled that the contract rate governs. And, as a practical matter, most oversecured creditors and their debtors simply assume that interest accrues postpetition at the same rate provided for by the note. But if the interest rate is unusually low, the banker may consider arguing for a higher postpetition rate to be set by the court. If the interest rate is high, the debtor argues the opposite.

If the bank is undersecured and the bank expects to suffer a deficiency after realization upon its collateral, then the claim of the bank *is split into two separate claims*—a secured claim and an unsecured claim. The secured claim is equal to the value of the collateral which secures the bank's debt and the unsecured claim is equal to the deficiency.

For example, two claims of the undersecured bank are illustrated below:

1. Total indebtedness of borrower	$3,500,000
Total value of bank's collateral	$2,000,000
Bank's deficiency	$1,500,000
2. The bank's secured claim	$2,000,000
The bank's unsecured claim	$1,500,000

These two different claims are treated differently, and many of these differences are highlighted in later portions of this book, particularly the treatment of a bank's unsecured and secured claims in a Chapter 11 plan of reorganization.

Concept of Value

The term "value" is not generally defined by the Bankruptcy Code, but it is a question that arises at several times in a case under the code. A determination of value at one stage of the case is not binding at another stage. But as a practical matter, the bankruptcy court is likely to remember previous contradictory evidence.

The first difficult factor in considering the concept of value is the standard of valuation. Should value be determined at the wholesale value, the retail value, the replacement value, the going concern value, the market value, or some other benchmark? The Bankruptcy Code leaves this issue for determination by the court. One bankruptcy court has found, for example, that in automatic stay litigation the standard value is "fair market value" if the debtor has a reasonable prospect for rehabilitation. It would seem to follow that where the debtor is not operating its business, the liquidation value would be more appropriate. One court has suggested that comparable sales provide the most appropriate standard of value for residential real estate.

Assuming that a standard of value appropriate to the facts of the bankruptcy case can be found, the next question is the date the value is to be determined. The possibilities include the date of the filing of the petition, the date of the hearing where value is an issue, the date of the hearing on confirmation of a plan of reorganization, etc. At least one court has held, in automatic stay litigation, that the date of valuation should be the date of the hearing, even where there was substantial evidence that the value of the collateral would be greatly increased within a short time following the hearing.

Concept of Adequate Protection

In bankruptcy cases, a creditor with an interest in property of the estate (a mortgage on the debtor's factory) is entitled to adequate protection of that property interest. Adequate protection is an elusive concept that depends on the particular facts of the case. The Bankruptcy Code does not define adequate protection, but provides examples of what may be considered adequate protection, including periodic cash payments; additional or replacement liens to protect a creditor from a decrease in value; or other, undefined measures which result in the secured creditor realizing the "indubitable equivalent" of its interest in the collateral. Obviously, the adequate protection which the bank needs varies from case to case, and even from time to time in the same case, and the lawyer and the banker must work closely to obtain the appropriate protection. The elusive concept of adequate protection is significant at several stages of any bankruptcy case.

Other Definitions

Insider

The Bankruptcy Code provides an extensive description of who is an insider of the debtor. Some insiders are specifically named. For example, if the debtor is an individual, his or her relatives and general partners, to name just a few, are insiders. If the debtor is a corporation, its officers and directors, among others, are insiders. Another specific provision of the code makes the bank an insider of the debtor if it indirectly owns, controls, or holds with power to vote 20% or more of the debtor's voting stock, *unless* the stock is held solely to secure a debt and the bank has not exercised the power to vote.

In addition to insiders who are specifically named by the statute (sometimes referred to as "statutory insiders"), there is another kind of insider—a person who is in control of the debtor.

Who is a person in control of the debtor? Does a bank become the person in control if it has the largest block of debt outstanding? Probably not, in the absence of other facts. What about the bank which, in a workout situation, dictates marketing strategy to the debtor? What if an employee of the bank periodically reviews all disbursements made by the debtor? What if the bank places an employee at the debtor's place of business and reviews each check before it is issued? What if the bank officer actually co-signs each check?

Is the bank a person in control if the affirmative and negative covenants in the loan documentation give the bank the complete power to control any significant aspect of the debtor's business, whether or not that right of control is exercised? Does a pledge of all the debtor's stock make the bank a person in control? Certainly, if the power to vote had not been exercised, and this was the only pertinent fact, the answer is no.

The determination of insider status is a question of fact. The banker who wishes to be "close" to the debtor must keep in mind the possible adverse consequences of becoming an insider.

A bank does not want to be the insider of a debtor in the bankruptcy court. A trustee may recover preferential payments to an insider for a period of one year prior to the filing of the petition, as compared with the 90-day period applicable to noninsiders. Sometimes the claims of insiders are subordinated to the claims of general creditors. Another reason to avoid the status of a "control person" or insider is to prevent later claims that the bank is responsible to the creditors for the demise of the debtor's business.

Debtor, Debtor in Possession, Trustee, Estate

In the Bankruptcy Code, the debtor is the individual, partnership, or corporation that files the bankruptcy case on its own behalf or has one filed against it in the case of an involuntary petition. In a Chapter 7 (liquidation) case, a trustee is appointed to collect and liquidate the assets of the debtor. In a Chapter 11 (reorganization) case, the debtor remains in possession of its property and is often referred to as the debtor in possession. The debtor in possession will "lose" possession and revert to a simple debtor if and when a trustee is appointed in the reorganization case. On the filing of the bankruptcy case, all the property interests of every kind of the debtor form the "estate."

Generally, when the Bankruptcy Code describes the powers or duties of a trustee in a Chapter 7 case, the reference is to the court appointed trustee and not the debtor. However, in a Chapter 11 case, the Bankruptcy Code may be referring either to the court-appointed trustee or the debtor in possession, because the debtor in possession has virtually every power and duty of the trustee in a Chapter 11 (reorganization) case. Thus, unless the context plainly requires otherwise, any discussion in this book about a Chapter 11 trustee is applicable to the debtor in possession.

Summary

On filing of a bankruptcy case, the automatic stay halts all collection efforts against the debtor, and sanctions for violating the automatic stay may include attorneys' fees and punitive damages.

Generally, interest stops accruing on unsecured claims on the filing of bankruptcy. However, oversecured creditors can collect postpetition interest as well as attorneys' fees and costs. A bank that is undersecured has two claims in bankruptcy: the secured claim, equal to the value of the collateral, and the unsecured claim, equal to the deficiency. Value, an important concept at several stages in a bankruptcy case, is undefined by the Bankruptcy Code, as is "adequate protection," another important concept.

From a pure bankruptcy law perspective, a bank does not want to be considered an insider of the debtor. The term is broadly defined and includes a person in control of the debtor. The bank's borrower is referred to as a debtor under the bankruptcy law, and in a Chapter 11 case, where no trustee has been appointed, is also a debtor in possession.

Liquidation Cases 11

Typically, in a Chapter 7 bankruptcy, the bank is concerned only with getting its collateral away from the clutches of the Bankruptcy Court. There are basically two ways to do this. One is to obtain an abandonment from the trustee and await the closing of the case. The other is to seek relief from the automatic stay. In some cases, the trustee has a right to sell the bank's collateral, and it may be necessary for the bank to protect itself from excessive costs incurred by the trustee in such a disposition.

Where the bank is undersecured, or completely unsecured, the bank can only participate in distributions made by the trustee by filing a proof of claim. Sometimes, because of the banker's knowledge of the debtor's affairs, he or she can be of assistance to the trustee in recovering preferential or fraudulent conveyances. In Chapter 7 cases concerning individuals, there are some additional concerns, which we discuss in chapter 14.

Recovery of Collateral

Abandonment and Closing of the Case

The automatic stay protects property "of the estate" only as long as property continues to be property of the estate. After an abandonment by the trustee, property is no longer property of the estate. Nevertheless, the automatic stay still protects it as property of the debtor, so an abandonment, in and of itself, does not free the property of the protection of the automatic stay.

In fact, where an abandonment is obtained, the automatic stay as to the debtor continues until the earliest of the following three events:

1. The time the case is closed.
2. The time the case is dismissed.
3. The time that a discharge is granted or denied, if the Chapter 7 case is a case concerning an individual.

Because a case may remain open for a considerable length of time, and because a discharge may be held up by complaints objecting to the debtor's discharge, this route to obtaining relief from the automatic stay is slow and uncertain. Its advantage is that little or no attorneys' fees will be generated. The faster route is described next.

Relief from the Automatic Stay

A secured creditor can obtain relief from the automatic stay by filing a motion in the bankruptcy court requesting that relief. The procedure is relatively simple; the elements of proof required, and the evidence to support those elements, may be straightforward or unusual.

Procedure

A motion to lift the automatic stay is just that—a motion filed in the bankruptcy court where the debtor's case is pending requesting that the court lift the automatic stay. If there has been an abandonment, the motion is only against the debtor. If there has not been an abandonment, then the motion should be filed against both the debtor and the trustee. The Bankruptcy Code provides that the court must have an initial hearing on a motion to lift the stay within 30 days from the date that it is filed. This usually means that the hearing is set down promptly.

At the preliminary hearing, the bankruptcy judge must lift the automatic stay unless the court orders the stay continued pending a final hearing. To make such a ruling, the court must find that there is a reasonable likelihood that the party opposing relief from the stay will prevail at the final hearing, and the final hearing must commence within 30 days of the preliminary hearing. The bankruptcy rules provide that the final hearing must be concluded within 30 days of its commencement.

The bankruptcy court has the discretion to hold the final hearing at the time the preliminary hearing is scheduled. In most cases, this is exactly what happens in Chapter 7 bankruptcies.

Elements of proof required to obtain relief

The court is required to terminate or modify the automatic stay either for "cause," which includes the lack of adequate protection of an interest in property or with respect to a stay relating to property, if the debtor does not have an equity in the property and the property is not necessary to an effective reorganization.

In the context of a Chapter 7 case, the second ground for obtaining relief from the automatic stay is simplified. Because a Chapter 7 case is nothing but a liquidation, property cannot be necessary to any effective reorganization. Thus, the only issue in a typical case in Chapter 7 is whether or not there is equity in the property. This determination is made by comparing the value of the collateral to the debt which is secured by the collateral. In most Chapter 7 cases, this is a relatively simple determination. Frequently, both the trustee and the debtor consent to the entry of an order lifting the stay.

Evidence

The evidence required at the hearing on the motion to lift the stay consists of two elements. Since equity is the question, the first matter is the amount of the debt. This process is no different from establishing a debt in an ordinary suit on a note, if there is a dispute. Often, however, there is no dispute, and the debtor has set forth the amount of the bank's debt in the schedules filed in the bankruptcy court.

The second aspect is proving value. There are many sources of evidence for this element. First, in the schedules, the debtor is required to make a statement as to the fair market value of the collateral. Sometimes the bank officer will be sufficiently familiar with the collateral that he or she can testify as to the fair market value. In other cases, such as automobiles, value may be established by reference to well known price digests, such as the Blue Book. If real estate is concerned, sometimes a broker testifies to value. But in other cases, a full-scale appraisal is necessary. Usually, the bank has a fairly current appraisal of real estate in the file, which can be updated for use at trial.

Sale of Collateral by a Trustee

Grounds

Generally, the trustee in a Chapter 7 case wants to sell the bank's collateral when there is equity over and above the bank's debt which can benefit the unsecured creditors. If there is such equity, the Bankruptcy Code authorizes the trustee to sell the property. As long as that process is not too drawn out, the bank should generally not care whether the trustee disposes of the property (thus paying off the debt) or whether the bank does that on its own.

There are other situations where the trustee has a right to sell the bank's collateral, including when the existence of the bank's lien is in bona fide dispute.

Protection from Excessive Costs

Where the trustee does have a right to sell the bank's collateral, the bank may need protection from excessive costs of sale. If the bank is amply oversecured, the costs incurred by the trustee in disposing of the property may be of little or no consequence, at least to the bank. However, in other cases, the bank may take appropriate action to be sure that the trustee does not charge more for disposition of the property than the bank would incur if it conducted its own foreclosure.

Participation in Case

Proof of Claim

If the bank is unsecured or partially unsecured, the only way it can participate in the distribution to unsecured creditors in a Chapter 7 case is by filing a proof of claim. The notice to creditors (which the bank should receive shortly after the filing of a petition) states the last day by which proof of claims may be filed. This deadline is strictly adhered to. For all practical purposes, if the bank files late, it will not get paid.

A proof of claim can generally be completed without much difficulty, and the banker familiar with bankruptcy should not need the assistance of counsel. However, if a loan officer does not routinely prepare proof of claim forms, it may be better to let an attorney handle the preparation and filing of the proof of claim. The proof of claim requires a statement of the amounts claimed, the consideration for the amounts claimed, and a statement as to the security, if any, which may be claimed for the debt. Attached to the proof of claim should be all notes, security agreements, financing statements, mortgages, or the like which evidence the claim or the security held for the claim.

The penalty for filing a false proof of claim is up to a $5,000 fine and up to five years in prison.

Assistance to Trustee Regarding Recovery of Preferences or Fraudulent Conveyances

From time to time, the banker knows enough about the borrower to know whether he or she has preferred any other creditors or if the debtor has made any conveyances which may be attacked as fraudulent. Other times, the bank simply has some strong suspicions about these matters. The trustee comes to the case totally ignorant of the debtor's business, its background, and transactions. To the extent that the debtor's records are complete and the trustee diligently examines them, the trustee should be able to discover obvious preferences or potential fraudulent conveyances.

However, this is not always a simple task and, even in moderate-size cases, could require sophisticated accounting help. Because preferences and fraudulent conveyances may go undetected by the trustee, it is important for the bank to educate the trustee concerning these possible recoveries. Of course, if the bank has some exposure itself, it probably wants to maintain a low profile.

Summary

In a Chapter 7 case, the usual desire of the bank officer is to get the collateral released from the automatic stay. This is generally accomplished by filing a motion for relief from the stay, which must be ruled on initially within 30 days. The stay may be lifted for cause or if the debtor has no equity in the property. Lack of equity is demonstrated by comparing the value of the collateral to the amount of the debt. If there is sufficient equity, the trustee has the right to sell the collateral. To receive a distribution as an unsecured creditor, the bank must file its proof of claim within the time set by the court.

Reorganization Cases 12

In contrast to the typical Chapter 7 case, a Chapter 11 case can present many different issues and many more complex matters of strategy. One fundamental concern is whether or not the bank believes the debtor has the ability to reorganize. Another critical area is the condition of the bank's collateral and whether or not it is declining in value. Assuming that the case proceeds to negotiation and proposal of a plan of reorganization, the ability of the debtor to "cram down" its intended plan on the bank must be carefully evaluated.

Working With or Against the Debtor

One of the first issues when a debtor files a Chapter 11 reorganization case is the bank's determination of the viability of the debtor's reorganization. This evaluation does not begin after the bankruptcy petition is filed. It is only a continuation of the evaluations which have been a part of the entire workout process. In some cases, this evaluation is strictly an economic one. Can the business make any money? Can the business make enough money given the amount of its debts? What will that mean for repayment to the bank? In other cases, the questions are wider in scope. Is the debtor honest? Has the debtor defrauded or otherwise intentionally harmed the bank?

Of course, the bank must consider the value and the condition of its collateral. If the value of the collateral can be established, how much equity cushion does the bank have? At the present rate of the debtor's losses, how long before that equity cushion will be eroded? At the present rate that interest is accruing, how long before the cushion is consumed? A review of all these and many other relevant factors is required before the bank can make the fundamental decision as to whether or not it wishes to work with the debtor in possession, and if so, on what terms.

Cash Collateral Use

In a Chapter 11 case, the debtor in possession remains in possession of its property. The Bankruptcy Code permits the debtor in possession to use its property in the ordinary course of its business, without seeking any authority from the court or creditors. There is, however, a significant limitation on the debtor's ability to use what is defined to be "cash collateral." Cash collateral is cash, negotiable instruments, documents of title, securities, deposit accounts, or other cash equivalents, including proceeds from collateral, in which the debtor and another entity (for example, the bank) have an interest. Under the Bankruptcy Code, the debtor in possession is not permitted to use cash collateral without obtaining the consent of the secured creditor who has rights in the cash collateral, or where the court, after notice to the creditor and a hearing, authorizes the debtor in possession to use cash collateral.

Thus, if the bank has significant amounts of cash collateral, such as an assignment of rents or a security interest in accounts receivable and proceeds, the bank may wish to remind the debtor (through debtor's counsel) that he or she is not permitted to use cash collateral without the bank's consent, lest there be any doubt that the bank does not consent to any use of cash collateral by the debtor. Sometimes debtors simply ignore this prohibition. In such cases, if the bank wants to press the issue, it has to go to court to seek an enforcement of this aspect of the bankruptcy laws.

What the debtor should do if it hasn't obtained the bank's consent is file a motion seeking either an ex parte hearing or one on very short telephonic notice, requesting the court's authorization to use cash collateral. Typically, the debtor alleges that it must use the cash collateral to support its operations; that its continued, uninterrupted operations are essential to its survivability as a going concern; that its existence as a going concern is critical to the realization of the maximum possible distribution to creditors and a successful reorganization. The debtor usually contends that the bank is adequately protected by the debtor's continued operations, which will (allegedly) create additional cash collateral for the protection of the bank. These arguments are generally persuasive to bankruptcy judges at the commencement of a case.

In such situations, the court usually authorizes the use of cash collateral, at least for a limited time. Generally, bankruptcy judges are unwilling to shut down the business of the new Chapter 11 debtor without the opportunity for a complete hearing, and some track record in the Chapter 11.

Conditions to Consent

Another common way to handle the issue is for the bank and the debtor to agree concerning the use of cash collateral and the protection given to the bank in exchange for the bank's consent. Among bankruptcy practitioners, this is sometimes referred to as "the dive." That is, in exchange for the right to use cash collateral, the debtor becomes a party to a consent order which confirms every penny of the lender's debt, the validity of each and every document which gives the lender a mortgage or security interest in the debtor's property and/or oldest child, and releases the lender from any and all liability of any nature whatsoever. It also gives the lender a security interest in all other collateral that it had not gotten before (for example, grandchildren).

There is at least one problem with this approach. Even where consent orders have been entered, at least one bankruptcy court has later declared such an agreement inoperative and unenforceable. Also, an alert creditors committee or its counsel will object to overbroad and overreaching agreements of this nature.

Certainly, however, consent orders of this type can serve legitimate ends. Thus, if the bank is looking to inventory, accounts receivable, and the proceeds of these categories as security, then it has a legitimate interest in the levels of inventory, the amount of accounts receivable, as well as the quality and age of specific receivables, and the amount of cash on hand. By establishing levels at which these values must be maintained, the bank has some benchmark by which to evaluate its situation as the debtor's operations continue. Moreover, the bank and the debtor can establish a consensual "standard" of adequate protection. If the debtor's financial situation deteriorates, the bankruptcy court has a less amorphous problem when it faces the question of whether or not the bank is adequately protected.

Of course, every loan has its own particular circumstances which dictate the conditions the bank decides to impose as a condition to its consent to the debtor's use of cash collateral. Experienced bankruptcy counsel can, of course, advise on those technical matters which must be addressed to fully protect the bank, including provisions that make clear the bank's secured position in postpetition collateral.

Use of Collateral Other than Cash

Where the bank's collateral is not cash collateral, the debtor may use it in the ordinary course of business, without any court order or any notice to the creditor. The debtor may also enter into transactions, such as the sale or lease of the bank's collateral, without notice or court approval, as long as the transaction is within the ordinary course of business. Thus, when the debtor is a manufacturing concern and the bank's security is the equipment used to manufacture goods, the debtor can continue business as usual after the filing and continue to operate the machinery. The limit on what a debtor can do is found in the phrase "ordinary course of business." A sale of such equipment would probably not be permitted, except on notice to the bank, with an opportunity to obtain a hearing.

The court must prohibit or condition such use, sale, or lease of collateral if the bank is not adequately protected. This issue usually arises in the context of a motion to lift the automatic stay, which is discussed in the next two sections of this chapter.

Relief from the Automatic Stay

The procedure for obtaining relief from the automatic stay in a Chapter 11 case is the same as in a Chapter 7 case. The elements of proof are different, however, and these are discussed in the following pages.

Elements of Proof Required to Obtain Relief

As discussed in connection with Chapter 7 cases, the bankruptcy court is required to terminate or modify the automatic stay either for "cause," which includes the lack of adequate protection of an interest in property or, with respect to a stay relating to property, if the debtor does not have an equity in the property and the property is not necessary to an effective organization.

Burden on Creditor

Because relief from the automatic stay is only available where the debtor has *no equity* in the collateral *and* where the *collateral is not necessary for an effective reorganization*, the difficulties facing the secured creditor in a Chapter 11 case are greater than in a Chapter 7 case. First, the Bankruptcy Code places the burden on the creditor to prove that there is no equity in the collateral. Obviously, just as in a Chapter 7 case, resolution of this question involves a comparison of the debt with the value of the collateral. Generally, in a Chapter 11 case, a going concern standard of valuation, rather than a liquidation or fire sale standard, most likely governs the court's analysis of value.

But even if the bank can prove that the debtor has no equity in the collateral, the court must also make a finding that the property is not necessary for an effective reorganization. Naturally, the debtor will claim that the bank's collateral is necessary to an effective reorganization. Whether or not this claim is justified is determined by the nature of the debtor's business, the degree to which the debtor is still in operation, the relationship of the collateral to the debtor's continued operations, and the intended plan of reorganization.

Collateral

Even where the debtor can demonstrate that the collateral is critical to continued operation of the business, and thus necessary to an effective reorganization, some courts have held that the bank can still satisfy this test if there is *no real prospect* for a *successful* reorganization. These courts hold that creditors are not required to forbear from realizing on their collateral if the prospects for a reorganization are but a mere will-o-the-wisp, or if there are no reasonable and real prospects for success. However, another court has looked to the provisions of the Bankruptcy Code which allow a business to liquidate while in Chapter 11 and has held that if the collateral is necessary to that liquidation, then this test is satisfied by the debtor, and the creditor cannot get relief from the stay.

Equity Cushion

Because of the added element of proof—that the property is not necessary to an effective reorganization—the other basis for relief from the automatic stay (for cause) becomes more important. Cause includes a lack of adequate protection. The issue of whether a creditor suffers from a lack of adequate protection is necessarily a question of fact. Where a bank is oversecured, the debtor typically asserts that the equity cushion available to the bank constitutes adequate protection. For the most part, courts recognize the existence of an equity cushion as a type of adequate protection, while conceding that equity cushions can dissipate quickly.

When a court finds that there is no equity cushion, or that the equity cushion which exists is insufficient to protect the bank, the debtor must give some other protection to the secured creditor. What is supposed to happen (although it doesn't always work this way) is that the debtor should make an offer to the bank of adequate protection. If the bank believes that the proposed protection is inadequate and presses its case to lift the stay, then the court must evaluate the "adequacy" of the adequate protection offered by the debtor. If the protection is not adequate, then the court should lift the automatic stay. If the protection is adequate, then the automatic stay remains in place. Some courts, however, will fashion *their own version* of adequate protection as a condition to the continuance of the automatic stay.

Of course, in cases involving property other than raw land, there are many factors other than the equity cushion. The bank also is concerned about whether or not insurance coverage is in place; whether or not the condition of the improvements is good; to what extent depreciation may occur with respect to the improvements, and other matters.

In one case, a bankruptcy court found that the creditor was adequately protected by a substantial equity cushion and noted that there was no evidence that the collateral (improved real property and personal property) was depreciating. In another case, however, the secured creditor was found to be adequately protected where there was little or no equity cushion, but where the debtor was making arrangements to preserve the status quo. The debtor did this by making payments to cover taxes and penalties which would be senior to the creditor's interest and by keeping the property properly insured and maintained. In another case, the bankruptcy court found that the creditor had an equity cushion which would not be eroded by the continuance of the automatic stay, because the debtor was paying monthly payments to the creditor in an amount sufficient to cover interest.

Where real property is collateral for the bank, both potential appreciation in value and fears of depreciation are factors in the court's analysis of whether or not the bank is adequately protected by the equity cushion. Where there is a willing buyer whose purchase of the property will satisfy the creditor's claim, the court is justified in not lifting the automatic stay, and, where there is an absence of a substantial buyer, the court may be inclined to lift the automatic stay.

Where the collateral consists of personal property, the same question of an equity cushion arises. And, of course, the bankruptcy courts can be expected to be concerned with the existence of adequate insurance coverage, maintenance of the property, and depreciation of the property. Although it is possible for personal property to appreciate, a secured creditor can usually contend that it is not adequately protected unless the debtor can compensate the secured creditor with "economic rent" to cover the depreciation resulting from the debtor's use or possession of the personal property. The amount of the economic rent depends on a multitude of facts, including the age of the property, its present condition, its use, and its remaining useful life.

Finally, the banker must not forget that the court only needs to find cause in order to lift the automatic stay. Where the legal or factual situation is out of the ordinary, the imaginative banker and counsel can assess the equities and make a case for relief even where all precedent is silent. Several courts have held that a lack of good faith in filing the bankruptcy case can, in itself, constitute grounds for relief from the automatic stay.

Obtaining Adequate Protection as Alternative Relief

Any banker seeking relief from the automatic stay should know that relief may not be granted. Accordingly, the bank should seek adequate protection for the bank's interest in its collateral as alternative relief from the court. Although the Bankruptcy Code permits the debtor in possession to use, sell, or lease property of the estate in the ordinary course of its business without an order of the court, that right is conditioned on the right of the secured creditor to receive adequate protection. As noted in our discussion of adequate protection in Chapter 10, the concept is one that is elusive and depends on the particular facts of the case. In the case of tangible personal property, the concept of economic rent is one which serves as a good example of adequate protection. Under the Bankruptcy Code, the court cannot grant the bank an administrative priority as adequate protection, because Congress recognized that the bankruptcy estate is not always able to satisfy even its administrative expenses.

The bank benefits in several ways from requesting adequate protection as alternative relief. First, if the bankruptcy court finds that the adequate protection offered is not sufficient, rather than lifting the stay, the court may choose to impose tougher terms on the debtor as a condition to keeping the automatic stay in force. If the debtor fails to meet the court-imposed burden, then the court will probably quickly lift the automatic stay.

Second, if the adequate protection ordered later turns out to be less than adequate when the case comes to an end, the bank can assert a "superpriority" administrative claim, which should be paid prior to almost all other administrative expenses of the Chapter 11 case. If the Chapter 11 case is not successful and is converted to a Chapter 7 case, even though the Chapter 7 administrative expenses generally have priority over those of Chapter 11, this superpriority claim will be paid before the administrative claims of the Chapter 7 case as well.

Debtor's Ability to Obtain Credit

A debtor in Chapter 11 frequently needs money, and one way is to borrow it. The Bankruptcy Code permits a debtor in possession to borrow money, but this authority is limited, depending on the circumstances. In effect, the Bankruptcy Code creates several levels of borrowing, with unsecured borrowing the easiest for the debtor to obtain, and secured borrowing, which supersedes secured creditors, the most difficult to obtain.

Unless the court orders to the contrary, a debtor in possession can obtain unsecured credit and incur unsecured debt in the ordinary course of its business, and the repayment is allowed as an administrative expense. Thus, if a debtor can find trade creditors that will extend unsecured credit, then no court order would be necessary to authorize the repayment of that trade credit, either through ongoing operations or in a plan of reorganization. This could be of concern where the bank has an unsecured claim and where any trade or other unsecured debt obtained by the debtor has a priority over the bank's claim and may diminish the assets available for creditors. So it must be kept in mind that, unless a creditor files a motion and the court orders that the debtor cannot incur unsecured credit, this power is available to the debtor.

Court Approval Needed

In cases where the debtor wishes to obtain unsecured credit, allowable as an administrative expense, which is *not* in the ordinary course of business, then the debtor must first seek and obtain court approval.

If the debtor is unable to obtain unsecured credit allowed as an administrative expense, then the debtor can ask the court to authorize borrowings secured by a lien on unencumbered property of the estate, or secured by a subordinate lien on property of the estate, or with priority over all administrative expenses.

Of course, sometimes the debtor cannot obtain credit under those conditions. Accordingly, the court can authorize the debtor to borrow money secured by a *senior or equal* lien on property of the estate that is already subject to a lien. But this can occur only if the debtor is unable to obtain credit otherwise and if there is adequate protection for the interest of the holder of the lien on the property on which the senior or equal lien is proposed to be granted. Obviously, the last thing a bank wants to happen is the loss of a first priority secured position. Before the debtor can gain court approval of financing secured by "priming" the bank, it must show that the bank will be adequately protected. The Bankruptcy Code places the burden of proof on the issue of adequate protection on the debtor.

Bank Protection

In those cases where the bank desires to lend money to the debtor, these procedures must be followed so that there is no question concerning the ability of the debtor (as a legal matter anyway) to repay the bank or to grant the bank security. In cases involving revolving credit or factoring arrangements, where the bank is secured primarily by accounts receivable, the debtor and the bank should structure their ongoing relationship in terms of borrowings by the debtor pursuant to court authorization. This would be analogous to the orders concerning the use of cash collateral discussed previously.

If the bank has agreed to lend money to the debtor in possession, and the court has authorized the lending arrangements, even if a party appeals that order, the bank is protected as to the validity of the debt and the lien or priority granted to the bank if it extends its credit in good faith, even though it is aware of a pending appeal. This is true unless, pending the appeal, a court stays the order which authorizes the loan.

Turnover of Repossessed Property

One of the more disheartening aspects of the Bankruptcy Code for many lenders is the provision concerning turnover. Turnover is a concept that affects the bank in several ways. The basic rule is that anyone who is in possession, custody, or control of property that the debtor may use, sell, or lease shall deliver it to the debtor, unless it is of inconsequential value or benefit to the estate. Even though the bank has taken possession of some or all of its collateral, if the debtor has rights in the collateral, such as a right to redeem, then the bank has a duty to give the collateral back.

However, since the bank is entitled to adequate protection for its interest in the property, it can usually insist on some form of adequate protection as a condition to returning the property.

Turnover arises in another important way when a depositor of a bank goes into bankruptcy. This is because the turnover provisions of the code require anyone who owes a debt to the debtor which is matured, payable on demand, or payable on order, to pay such debt to the trustee. This is subject to one important exception: The debt is subject to an offset in favor of the bank, which is discussed below.

Offset

Even when there is no offset to be considered, this portion of the Bankruptcy Code can present some problems of interpretation for the bank. If the debtor has filed a Chapter 7 case, then a trustee is appointed immediately, and as soon as the bank knows of the bankruptcy case, it is a simple matter to transfer the funds to the trustee. Where the debtor files a Chapter 11, and there is no offset to be considered, the only entity to whom the bank could give the money in the account would be the debtor in possession since, ordinarily, no trustee would be appointed.

Problems arise, however, in Chapter 13 cases where the bank is aware of the filing of the case. There, the debtor remains in possession of the estate, yet a trustee is appointed. In this situation, a bank may find itself subjected to competing claims to the money.

In most cases, a bank does not know that one of its checking account customers has gone into bankruptcy, unless the customer also owes money to the bank because the notice sent by the court is only directed to creditors. As long as the bank has neither actual notice nor actual knowledge of the commencement of the bankruptcy case, the bank cannot be held liable for honoring the debtor's checks in good faith.

To the extent that the bank has rights of offset, the obligation of turnover does not apply. However, the bank must be cautious in preserving its right of offset on the one hand, but not violating the automatic stay by *consummating* the offset. The courts have handed down some contradictory decisions concerning just how a bank should or can preserve its right of offset by freezing the account and yet not violate the automatic stay. In such situations, counsel should be consulted as to local practice or governing law in the district where the case is pending.

Appointment of a Trustee or Examiner and Conversion or Dismissal of a Case

When it is apparent that the continuance of the debtor as debtor in possession is not in the best interest of the bank, consideration should be given to appointing a trustee or examiner, or, depending on the circumstances, seeking conversion of the case to a Chapter 7, or dismissal of the case.

The Bankruptcy Code provides, on request of a party, that the court *shall* order the appointment of a trustee, either for cause or if such appointment is in the interest of creditors. Cause specifically includes "fraud, dishonesty, incompetence, or gross mismanagement of the affairs of the debtor *by current management*, either before or after the commencement of the case, or similar cause." By way of comparison, the court may convert a Chapter 11 case to a Chapter 7 case or may dismiss a case, whichever is in the best interest of creditors and the estate, for cause. Here, cause includes:

- Continuing loss to or diminution of the estate and absence of a reasonable likelihood of rehabilitation.
- Inability to effectuate a plan.
- Unreasonable delay by the debtor that is prejudicial to creditors.
- Failure to propose a plan within the time fixed by the court.
- Denial of confirmation of every proposed plan and denial of additional time for filing another plan or a modification of a plan.

After a plan is confirmed, the court may convert or dismiss the case on revocation of an order of confirmation and denial of confirmation of another plan or a modified plan; inability to effectuate substantial confirmation of a confirmed plan; material default of the debtor with respect to a confirmed plan; and termination of a plan through occurrence of a condition specified in the plan.

Obviously, there may be cases in which the facts support either a trustee or a conversion or dismissal of the case, because incompetence or gross mismanagement would most likely lead to loss and diminution of the estate, as well as the inability to propose or effectuate a plan.

As a general rule, in situations where the management of the debtor is dishonest or engaging in a fraud, the bank likes an independent trustee to take over the assets of the business, so that further dishonesty can be stopped. If the management is honest but inept, the bank may prefer simply to have the case dismissed so that the automatic stay expires and foreclosure proceeds. Alternatively, the bank may prefer conversion to a Chapter 7 so those assets not yet dissipated by management inefficiency can be distributed to the creditors.

One less severe alternative available to a court where there are allegations of fraud, dishonesty, incompetence, misconduct, mismanagement, or irregularity in the management of the debtor's affairs is the appointment of an examiner. If such allegations are made in a case where the debtor's unsecured debts (other than certain debts, including debts owed to insidders) exceed $5 million, then the appointment of an examiner is automatic. The examiner will investigate the claims of misconduct.

Creditors Committee

In every Chapter 11 case, the court is directed to appoint a committee of creditors holding unsecured claims. Ordinarily, that committee consists of the persons who are willing to serve, who hold the seven largest claims against the debtor of the kinds represented on such committee, or the members of the committee organized by creditors before the case is filed, if that committee was fairly chosen and represents the different kinds of claims to be represented. The court can appoint additional persons to the committee and can also appoint other committees to represent other interests in the case.

With the approval of the court, a creditors committee may employ attorneys or accountants to represent or assist it. The committee may:

• Consult with the trustee or the debtor concerning the administration of the case.

• Investigate the acts, conduct, assets, liabilities, and financial condition of the debtor, the operation of the debtor's business and the desirability of its continuance, and any other matter relevant to the case or the formulation of a plan.

• Participate in the formulation of a plan, advise those represented by the committee of such committee's determination as to any plan formulated, and collect and file with the court acceptances or rejections of the plan; request the appointment of a trustee or examiner; and perform such other services in the interest of those represented.

If the bank holds the distinction of having enough debt to be appointed to the creditors committee, it should not remain on the committee unless it intends to be active. If it does not intend to serve, either because the case itself is not that large and the bank does not wish to devote the time required to serve on the committee, or for other reasons, the bank should affirmatively inform the court that it is not willing to serve on the committee. Committee members do have fiduciary responsibilities, and there is no reason to risk that someone would later contend that those duties were improperly or inadequately discharged. If the bank is involved in a case where its claim and the case are large enough to warrant participation on the committee, it should attend the meetings of the committee, and act in good faith on behalf of the claims represented by the committee.

Often, the bank's unsecured claim is the result of the bank having a deficiency claim after consideration of the amount of the debt outstanding and the value of the collateral available to it. In such cases, the bank's interests are necessarily adverse to those of the unsecured creditors in general. Accordingly, the other creditors may not particularly wish to have the bank serve on the committee. The bank, because of its divided loyalties which result from its concern for its secured position and for its treatment of its unsecured position, may not wish to serve on the committee.

The creditors committee can take a very strong leadership role in some Chapter 11 cases and often can gain the ear of the bankruptcy judge where individual creditors might not. The counsel for the committee may be paid from the debtor's estate, which lessens the direct burden on the bank and the other creditors that would otherwise have to bear their attorneys' fees in connection with the case.

The goal of a Chapter 11 debtor is to propose and have confirmed a plan of reorganization which extends the time in which the debtor must pay the debts and/or reduce the amount of some of those debts. The goal of the creditors is to get paid as much as possible as soon as possible. The Bankruptcy Code is structured to encourage these conflicting interests to bargain and to arrive at a compromise.

At one extreme, the debtor says to the unsecured creditors: If I have to liquidate, you won't get anything. If you let me stay in business, I can pay you something over time.

The unsecured creditors reply: You can't retain your ownership interest unless you pay us enough so that we vote in favor of your plan. The Bankruptcy Code does not allow you to ignore us.

The debtor says to the secured creditors: Your collateral is not worth near what you think it is, nor is it worth anything like the amount of debt I owe you, so your claim is split into an unsecured claim and a secured claim. As to your secured claim, I will pay you over time what your collateral is worth, including interest.

The secured creditor replies: The collateral is worth more than my debt, and you must pay me all of it, including my attorneys' fees, with a market rate of interest.

In this chapter, the specific rules that govern confirmation of a plan, and this bargaining process, are covered. But before diving into the rules governing confirmation, let's review the process by which a plan is proposed to the creditors.

Proposal of Plan and Submission of Disclosure Statement

The process by which a plan is proposed and submitted to the creditors for a vote is relatively straightforward. The person who proposes the plan is known as the proponent and is usually the debtor. The debtor prepares a written plan of reorganization which he or she must file with the court. In the plan, the debtor classifies claims, describes the proposed treatment of the various classes of claims, and sets forth the means for the plan's execution. In addition to the plan of reorganization, the proponent must also file a written disclosure statement. Similar in purpose to a proxy statement, the disclosure statement is designed to furnish creditors with adequate information so they can make an informed decision to vote for or against the plan.

After the plan and the disclosure statement have been filed with the clerk of the bankruptcy court, the bankruptcy court sends out a notice to all creditors setting a date for the hearing on the disclosure statement. Typically, creditors who wish to review the disclosure statement must obtain their own copies from the court at this point in the proceedings. The court is required by the Bankruptcy Code to have a hearing to approve or disapprove the disclosure statement, and the proponent cannot solicit votes for the plan until such time as the disclosure statement has been approved and transmitted to creditors.

If the bank has an unsecured claim and opposes acceptance and confirmation of a plan, the bank will want to be sure that the disclosure statement contains all the information about the debtor which has led the bank to conclude that the plan should not be accepted or confirmed. The debtor may not want the disclosure statement to contain the same information. If the debtor has not made a disclosure of "adequate information" to his creditors, the bank should consider objecting to the approval of the disclosure statement. The reported decisions show that the courts require disclosure statements to include detailed information as a condition to their approval.

Once the disclosure statement has been approved, both the disclosure statement and the plan or a summary of the plan are transmitted to all creditors, with a notice from the court. In the notice, the court sets a date by which votes on the plan must be filed; a date by which any objection to confirmation must be filed; and a date for the confirmation hearing itself.

The bank must submit its vote in a timely fashion in order for it to be counted. If the bank wishes to help defeat or gain approval of the plan of reorganization, it may consider soliciting other creditors for their votes. As noted, this cannot be done until the disclosure statement has been approved and transmitted to all creditors.

The bank's lawyer should carefully review the plan to see if it meets the 11 requirements of confirmation. If it does not, a written objection must be filed if the bank wishes to oppose confirmation. At the confirmation hearing, the bank must be prepared to put on its evidence in opposition to confirmation. After the hearing, the court either confirms the plan or denies confirmation. If the plan is confirmed, it becomes the blueprint under which the debtor operates. An appeal from the order confirming the plan will not stay performance under the plan, unless a supersedeas order is obtained.

The 11 Conditions to Confirmation

The Bankruptcy Code generally provides that a plan shall be confirmed only if 11 requirements are met. While all these requirements are important, the eighth is particularly important, because of its connection with the process of cram down. Accordingly, the eighth is treated last. These 11 requirements make up the checklist that the bankruptcy judge must use to evaluate a plan at the confirmation hearing.

Requirement No. 1

The plan must comply with the applicable provisions of the Bankruptcy Code. For instance, the plan must designate classes of claims and specify their treatment; provide for the same treatment of each claim in a class, unless the holder of a particular claim agrees to a less favorable treatment; and provide adequate means for the plan's execution. Claims can only be classed together if they are substantially similar. If the debtor is a corporation, the charter must be amended as to certain technical matters regarding the issuance of securities and allocation of voting power among classes.

Requirement No. 2

The proponent of the plan *must have complied with the applicable provisions* of the Bankruptcy Code. Usually, the proponent is the debtor, and there are many provisions of Chapter 11 and other chapters which govern the conduct of the debtor. As an example, if the debtor had not filed his or her schedules or did not file periodic reports with the court regarding financial condition, the court could bar confirmation on that basis. If the debtor had used the bank's cash collateral without the bank's consent and without court authorization, the court might be persuaded to deny confirmation.

Requirement No. 3

The *plan* must have been *proposed in good faith* and not by any means forbidden by law. Good faith is a nebulous concept in bankruptcy law, and it is undergoing development. The banker and the banker's lawyer must consider whether facts exist which might warrant a finding that the debtor's plan was not proposed in good faith. If such facts exist, the court may be convinced that confirmation should be denied.

Requirement No. 4

Any payment made or to be made by the debtor (or certain other parties) for services or expenses in connection with the case or the plan *has been approved by or is subject to the approval of the court as reasonable.*

Requirement No. 5

The proponent of the plan must have *disclosed the identity and affiliation of any individual proposed to serve* after confirmation *as a director, officer, or voting trustee* of the debtor (or an affiliate or successor of the debtor). The appointment to (or continuance) in such office of such individual must be consistent with the interest of creditors and equity security holders and with public policy. In addition, the proponent of the plan must have disclosed the identity of any insider who will be employed or retained by the reorganized debtor and the nature of any compensation for such insider. These disclosures should have been made in the disclosure statement regarding the plan, but the determination of whether these appointments are consistent with the interest of creditors and with public policy must necessarily await the confirmation hearing.

Requirement No. 6

Where applicable, the sixth requirement is that any governmental *regulatory commission* with jurisdiction over the rates of the debtor *has approved any rate change* provided for in the plan, or such rate change is expressly conditioned on such approval.

Requirement No. 7

This requirement is known as the "best interest of creditors" test. Simplified, this test says that as to each impaired class, *each holder of a claim* in that class *has either accepted* the plan *or will receive* or retain under the plan *as much as he or she would receive* or retain if the debtor were liquidated *under Chapter 7*. (There is a variation of this rule that is important where the secured creditor has made what is known as the Section 1111(b)(2) election, which is discussed later in this book.) So, whenever the debtor wants to pay a creditor less than the creditor could get in a Chapter 7, even if every other creditor involved were to vote in favor of the plan, the single creditor who had not accepted the plan and who could demonstrate to the court that he or she would do better in a Chapter 7 will be able to block confirmation. This would require a valuation of the debtor's assets as of the effective date of the plan and requires comparison to the treatment of claims proposed under the plan. This is a very different test from Requirement No. 8, which is concerned with the treatment of a *class* that has not accepted the plan. Requirement No. 7 focuses on the treatment of a *single* nonaccepting, impaired creditor. The concept of impairment is discussed below.

Requirement No. 9

This deals with the treatment of certain administrative or *tax claims* and ordinarily would not be the type of claims which would affect the bank directly.

Requirement No. 10

At least *one class of impaired claims must have accepted the plan*. This test must be met without including the votes in favor of the plan by any insider holding a claim in the accepting class. This test requires the debtor to find some class of creditors willing to vote for the plan even though its claims are being impaired.

Requirement No. 11

The final requirement is that confirmation of the plan is *not likely to be followed by the liquidation, or the need for further financial reorganization*, of the debtor or any successor to the debtor under the plan, *unless such liquidation or reorganization is proposed in the plan itself*. This requirement can be the basis of considerable factual inquiry and testimony of experts and, of course, focus on the economic performance of the debtor and the market-place in which the debtor operates.

Requirement No. 8

We now turn to the eighth requirement. If each of the 11 requirements for confirmation is met, the court can confirm the plan. There will be no cram down. Requirement No. 8 is important because if each of the 11 requirements for confirmation is met, *other than Requirement No. 8*, the plan can only be confirmed if the court is permitted to cram down the plan.

Each class must have accepted the plan or such class is not impaired under the plan.

• Has the class accepted the plan? Whether or not a class has accepted the plan is easily determined. If two-thirds in amount of debt and one-half in number of creditors voting in a particular class has accepted the plan, that class has accepted the plan. Otherwise, it has rejected the plan. Generally, the holder of a secured claim will be in a class all by itself. If a class rejects the plan, Requirement No. 8 is met only if that class is not "impaired" under the plan.

• Is the rejecting class impaired? A class is impaired if, for example, the plan proposes to pay 50¢ on the dollar or a payment of 100¢ on the dollar on prepetition, matured, and payable debt is stretched out over a four-year period. The Bankruptcy Code defines it this way: A class is impaired *unless* the plan does one of three things.

1. The plan can leave unaltered the legal, equitable, and contractual rights to which the claim entitles the claimant. That would mean that the claimants of that class could bring suit, enforce judgments, and the like, the very thing that most Chapter 11 debtors file bankruptcy to avoid.

2. The plan can provide that, on the effective date of the plan, the claimant receives cash equal to the allowed amount of the claim. That's simple: immediate payment in full.

3. Certain claims may be "de-accelerated." This provision of the code is important in the case of a long-term debt because it gives the debtor a chance to put back into place a long-term loan or mortgage which has favorable terms, even though the debtor had previously gone into default. To de-accelerate a claim, the debtor must do four things.

1. The debtor must cure any defaults that occurred before or after the commencement of the case.

2. The plan must reinstate the maturity of the debt as it existed before default.

3. The debtor must compensate the bank for any damages it incurred as a result of any reasonable reliance on the right to acceleration.

4. The plan cannot otherwise alter the legal, equitable, or contractual rights of the bank.

If a class of claims rejects the plan and that class is impaired under the plan, Requirement No. 8 is not satisfied. If all these 11 requirements are met, the court can confirm the plan. If each one of these elements is met except for the eighth—that is, each class has accepted the plan or any rejecting class is not impaired under the plan—the debtor will ask the court to cram down the plan on the rejecting class.

Process of Cram Down

The term cram down does not appear in the Bankruptcy Code. Instead, the Bankruptcy Code states where all the requirements of confirmation are met other than Requirement No. 8, the court shall nevertheless confirm the plan *if the plan does not discriminate unfairly and is fair and equitable* with respect to each rejecting, impaired class.

For the bank's purposes, this situation can arise in two different contexts. First, where the bank is a secured creditor, the bank will generally be in a class by itself. If it votes against the treatment proposed under the plan, then as to its secured claim, the court will look to see if the treatment is "fair and equitable."

In the second case, where the bank has an unsecured claim and the unsecured claims are impaired but have not accepted the plan, the court will look to see if the unsecured class is treated fairly and equitably.

The concept of what is fair and equitable is not left to the imagination of the bankruptcy judge. Instead, the Bankruptcy Code sets out different specific standards which are applicable to secured claims or unsecured claims. These specific standards seem more complex than they really are. One must work through the several aspects of these tests with examples before the meaning can be grasped.

Cram Down of a Class of Secured Claims

For a class of secured claims, the condition that the plan be fair and equitable can be satisfied in one of three ways. The first way is the most common test applied: The plan will be fair and equitable if the secured creditor retains its lien securing its claim and receives on account of its claim deferred cash payments totaling at least the allowed amount of such claim, having a present value (as of the effective date of the plan) of at least the value of the collateral.

Cash payments

There are a number of complex concepts tied up in this first test. Remember that the claim of the bank (where undersecured) will be split in two claims—the secured claim, which is equal to the value of the collateral, and an unsecured claim, to the extent that the bank is unsecured or has a deficiency claim. So, if the bank is owed $3.5 million and the collateral is worth $2 million, the bank has a secured claim of $2 million and an unsecured claim of $1.5 million. The unsecured claim is not considered by the court in determining the fair and equitable treatment of the bank's secured claim (unless the Section 1111(b) election is made which is discussed later). So in this example, the plan must state that the bank retains its lien in the collateral.

Next, the bank must receive deferred cash payments totaling at least the allowed amount of such claim. That means that the face amount of the money to be paid to the bank would have to equal or exceed $2 million. In our example, annual payments of $200,000 for 10 years would satisfy this part of the test. But would 10 payments of $200,000 spread over 10 years have a value of $2 million? Of course not, especially in today's inflationary economy.

This problem is addressed in the next element of the "fair and equitable" test. This aspect requires that the deferred cash payments have a present value, determined as of the effective date of the plan, of at least the value of the bank's collateral. Here, that would mean that the deferred cash payments *must have a present value* of $2 million.

In our example, the plan could not be confirmed if the debtor had proposed to repay this $2-million secured claim over 10 years at $200,000 a year, with no interest. Although the deferred cash payments would total the allowed amount of the claim, the present value of those deferred cash payments would not equal the value of the collateral. To be confirmable, the debtor would have to pay interest at an appropriate rate, so that when a discount rate is applied to the proposed payments of principal and interest, the present value of the deferred cash payments will equal $2 million.

Under this test, could the debtor cram down this treatment on the bank: 10 annual payments of $325,000 with the first payment due one year after confirmation of the plan? Obviously, the first half of the test is met: the face amount of the payments equals or exceeds the $2-million allowed secured claim. But is the present value of this stream of payments equal to $2 million now? The answer, of course, depends on the discount rate which is applied to this stream of payments. If the discount rate is 12.5%, the present value is less than $2 million (in fact, it comes to $1,799,340). If the discount rate is 9%, then these payments are worth more than $2 million ($2,085,738.80).

Generally speaking, courts equate the discount rate to the interest rate that a lender would charge to make a loan in the amount of the claim and for the time period proposed by the plan, given the security for repayment and the other risks.

The upshot is that the bank's secured claim must be paid in full. Obviously, the bank must convince the court to apply an appropriate interest rate. Also, the way this test works means that the bank will want the court to find its collateral to have the greatest possible value at confirmation. The debtor will want the opposite result. (This is a reversal of the positions that the parties might have taken in connection with automatic stay litigation.) Where there is a dispute as to valuation, the bankruptcy court has to conduct a valuation hearing either before or in connection with the confirmation hearing.

Sale of collateral

The second method by which the debtor may satisfy the fair and equitable test for a secured claim is to provide for the sale of the collateral free and clear of the lien, with the lien to attach to the proceeds of the sale. The disposition of the proceeds to satisfy the lien must be consistent with the test just described, or consistent with the third test, described below.

The third and final test for confirmation of a plan over the objection of a secured creditor is whether the plan provides for the realization by the secured creditor of the "indubitable equivalent" of its claim. This clause is designed to allow some flexibility and yet maintain a high standard of protection for the secured creditor.

Cram Down of the Unsecured Class

In the case of the class of unsecured claims, there is a totally different test of what is fair and equitable. To continue with our example, the bank has an unsecured claim of $1.5 million. Assume that all other unsecured claims total $2.9 million. In such a situation, the bank controls the unsecured class, because if it votes "no" with respect to the proposed treatment of unsecured creditors, the affirmative vote by every other unsecured creditor would not total two-thirds in amount. So, assume that the debtor proposed payment of 30¢ on the dollar over six years to all unsecured creditors, and the bank rejected that treatment. As a result, an impaired class would not have accepted the plan, and, accordingly, the plan could not be confirmed (even if all other classes had accepted the plan), unless the debtor can cram down this treatment.

For a plan to be fair and equitable with respect to a nonaccepting impaired unsecured class, the plan must provide *either* that each holder in the class receive or retain on account of such claim property having a present value (as of the effective date of the plan) equal to the allowed amount of the claim *or* the holder of any claim or interest that is junior to the claim of such class will not receive or retain on account of such junior claim or interest any property. In short, the unsecured class must be paid in full (immediately or over time, with the discount rate considered) or the owner must not retain or receive any property.

This test brings in sharp focus the negotiation that the Bankruptcy Code encourages between the debtor and the unsecured creditors. The debtor is saying that the business has too much debt to survive, but if he *keeps the business* he *can pay a part* of the indebtedness and that is better than nothing. If the unsecured creditors do not believe that the debtor is making the best effort to pay as much as is reasonably possible under the circumstances, they can reject the proposed treatment. If, *as a class*, they reject the proposed treatment, the debtor cannot receive or retain any property if he wants the plan confirmed.

If the debtor cannot retain an ownership interest, there is no incentive to seek confirmation. If 30¢ on the dollar is, in fact, the best that the debtor can do and the creditors will not receive that much in a liquidation, then their sense of self-interest should cause them to vote in favor of the plan. If they think the debtor can do better, they have strong leverage to seek a higher payout. If they ask too much and block confirmation, they will get whatever liquidation ultimately provides.

The courts have created one exception to this rather strict requirement. In essence, the courts have said that the debtor can repurchase the ownership interest if the debtor provides substantial new funds to acquire or retain an ownership interest. What is substantial under the circumstances of the case varies, but the cases are clear that a nominal or token payment is not sufficient.

That is what cram down is. Generally, cases just do not get that far. The intent of the drafters of the code—that the debtor negotiate with its creditors as classes—has apparently occurred because there is a lack of reported cases where cram down issues are resolved.

Section 1111(b) Election

From time to time, mention has been made of the Section 1111(b) election. Section 1111 of the code is complex and shadowed in mystery, even to experienced bankruptcy practitioners. But if some restrictions and conditions on Section 1111 are put aside and some practical applications of Section 1111 are described, the banker can get a reasonable feel of what is involved in the Section 1111(b) election. Before explaining the Section 1111(b) *election*, the Section 1111(b) *effect* must be explained.

Section 1111(b) cannot be understood unless one keeps in mind the Bankruptcy Code's concept that the undersecured creditor has two claims, one which is a secured claim up to the value of the collateral and the other which is an unsecured claim, equal to the creditor's deficiency. In certain lending situations, lenders have made nonrecourse loans or property has been purchased subject to mortgage indebtedness. The Section 1111(b) effect is limited to these situations. Where a nonrecourse loan is extended or property is purchased subject to a mortgage, the borrower has no personal liability on the note. If the borrower is unable to repay the amounts due under a nonrecourse loan, the bank can look only to the collateral to collect its indebtedness. To simplify somewhat, the effect of Section 1111(b) is that, for the purposes of bankruptcy, a claim is treated as if the bank had recourse against the debtor, *whether or not* the bank has recourse under state law.

Thus, because of the language of Section 1111, if this $3.5-million debt of the bank was based on a nonrecourse loan to the debtor, the bank would have its secured claim of $2 million and would also be treated *as though it* had a recourse claim for the deficiency. This would allow the bank to vote its deficiency claim, which might give it considerable clout in blocking an unfavorable plan of reorganization, as is discussed above.

In the absence of these provisions of Section 1111(b), the debtor could pay off the secured claim (equal to $2 million) and walk away from the $1.5-million deficiency. After confirmation, the bank would be unable to hope for future appreciation of its collateral as a source of repayment because the value would be fixed as of the date of confirmation. Thus, the Section 1111(b) effect puts the nonrecourse lender on the same footing as the recourse lender for purposes of bankruptcy.

The Section 1111(b) election is available to a bank whether its loan to the debtor was recourse or nonrecourse. In our example, the bank has a $2-million "allowed secured claim" and a $1.5-million "allowed unsecured claim." Making the election changes the bank's "allowed secured claim" to the full face amount of the claim ($3.5 million), rather than the value of the collateral ($2 million). Thus, if the bank made the Section 1111(b) election, its allowed secured claim would be $3.5 million and *it would not have any unsecured claim*. Now, in our example, that might not be the best strategy to adopt, because by making the Section 1111(b) election, the bank would *give up its control* of the unsecured class. That control can result in tremendous leverage over a debtor and should not be lightly forsaken.

However, change the example to assume that the case is a much larger one, and the total of the other unsecured debt is $150 million. In such a case, the bank's deficiency claim cannot control the unsecured class. Assume also that the plan of reorganization proposes to pay unsecured creditors a very small percentage payout, at some time in the future, which will not have much value to the bank. To understand the possible benefit of making the 1111(b) election, we must compare the treatment of the bank's secured claim under the standards of cram down.

If the Section 1111(b) election is made, the allowed secured claim would be $3.5 million and the face amount of the payments made to the bank would have to equal $3.5 million (rather than $2 million, plus "interest" on the $2-million claim). However, this stream of payments totaling $3.5 million would still only have to have a present value of $2 million, the value of the collateral. Why would this election be beneficial? If the treatment of unsecured creditors was such that there would be no significant return to the bank, and the bank thought that the debtor would ultimately default under the plan, permitting the bank to foreclose, then the bank could foreclose its full debt. Otherwise, it might foreclose with only a $2-million debt, and if the property had appreciated, some equity might have to be returned to the debtor.

The circumstances where this election might be beneficial depend on the facts of the case, and the banker and the lawyer need to carefully assess the debtor's circumstances and the possible proposed plans in considering this election.

Other Considerations 14

The question often arises: does it make sense for the bank to put the debtor into an involuntary bankruptcy, and, if that is a desirable goal, what does it take to accomplish it?

Involuntary Bankruptcies

The bank may protect its self-interest by bringing a lawsuit and endeavoring to collect from the debtor. Of course, if the debtor ultimately goes into bankruptcy within 90 days of the date that the bank is paid, or obtains a judgment, or receives some other collateral, those transfers may ultimately be set aside as preferential, depending on the facts. But as long as the bank is not an insider, once the 90-day period has elapsed, at least under bankruptcy law, there will be no ground for a recovery of that transfer. So, the bank's first desire should be to protect itself and to get its loan repaid. The fear that payments may later be recovered as preferential is not a reason to ignore collection of the debt. Collect now, and let the lawyer worry about defending the preference suit later. Keep in mind that realization on the bank's collateral is not preferential.

If, on the other hand, the bank suspects or knows that the debtor is paying other creditors and is not paying the bank, then the bank is rightfully concerned about the preferential effect of those transfers. Unless state law offers a remedy, the bankruptcy law is the only way that these preferential payments can be recovered for the benefit of the bank and other creditors of the debtor. Obviously, if the bank has received a payment or other transfer within the 90-day (or, where applicable, one year) preference period, it will not want to initiate an involuntary bankruptcy.

Similarly, even if the debtor is not preferring creditors but is dishonest and is making fraudulent conveyances which enrich the officers, directors, or relatives of the debtor, then the bank may benefit from a bankruptcy. In bankruptcy, a trustee is appointed to protect and recover the assets of the estate for the benefit of the creditors. Counsel should be consulted to determine if state law remedies may be more beneficial to the bank.

Procedure

Once the decision has been made to bring an involuntary petition, if the debtor has a total of 12 or more creditors, the bank must find 2 other petitioning creditors. Where the debtor has fewer than 12 creditors, the bank can file an involuntary petition by itself, as long as the other requirements are met.

Once the requisite number of petitioning creditors is assembled, if their combined unsecured, noncontingent, and undisputed debt equals at least $5,000 and the debtor is generally not paying his or her debts as they come due (other than debts which are in bona fide dispute), then the petition can be filed. If the debtor disputes the allegation that it is not paying debts as they come due, the court sets the matter down for a prompt hearing, and discovery can be commenced.

Costs and Risks

If the debtor has disputed the involuntary petition and has prevailed, the court may grant a judgment against the petitioning creditors for the debtor's costs, reasonable attorneys' fees, and, where applicable, for any damages caused by taking possession of the debtor's property by a trustee appointed by the court. And if any petitioner filed a petition in bad faith, the court may award damages caused by the filing or punitive damages, or both.

It is important to understand that the filing of an involuntary petition in and of itself does not mean that a trustee automatically takes over the debtor's property. No "order for relief" will be entered until the debtor defaults by not answering the petition or after the court has held a hearing on whether or not the debtor is generally not paying debts, other than debts in bona fide dispute, as they become due. During this gap, the petitioning creditors may request the court to appoint an interim trustee to preserve the property of the estate or to prevent loss to the estate. The Bankruptcy Code permits the debtor to regain possession of the property in the possession of the trustee prior to the entry of an order for relief, if the debtor files such bond as the court may require to protect the property of the estate.

Cases Concerning Individuals

Where the debtor is an individual, there are some special provisions of the Bankruptcy Code which are important and are discussed in the following pages.

Exemptions

Debtors are entitled to claim exemptions when they file a bankruptcy case. This is to further the policy of the debtor receiving a fresh start after the bankruptcy is completed. So, instead of all the debtor's earthly belongings irrevocably becoming the property of the trustee for disposition, the debtor claims as exempt those items believed to be exempt under state or federal law. The federal bankruptcy law offers a fairly generous exemption to a debtor, and in the case of a husband and wife who are joint debtors, both may claim the federal exemption, or both may claim the state exemption but one cannot choose the federal exemption and the other choose the state exemption. However, Congress did authorize states to "opt out" of the federal exemption scheme and provide debtors of their state with exemptions created under state law. Many states have done so, and the bank's counsel can advise as to the exemptions allowed in the appropriate state.

A creditor is required to object to property claimed as exempt within a very short time frame, so it is important to examine the schedules filed by the debtor promptly. If any improper exemptions are claimed, it is important to file timely objections to protect the rights of the bank.

Fraudulent Conveyances

Experience indicates that cases concerning individuals are more likely to be ones where fraudulent conveyances have occurred to the detriment of creditors. The debtor is required to state, under penalty of perjury, those transfers made within the one-year period prior to bankruptcy. If the debtor is truthful, this information can be the basis for discovering and ultimately recovering a fraudulent conveyance.

In a Chapter 7 case, it is the trustee's job to pursue fraudulent conveyances for the benefit of all creditors. Sometimes, trustees are not willing or feel that they are unable to afford the lengthy proceedings required to recover fraudulent transfers. Creditors can get authority from the bankruptcy court in these situations to bring fraudulent conveyance actions for the benefit of all creditors, and this may be an appropriate option to pursue.

Discharge and Dischargeability Litigation

The ultimate benefit of bankruptcy is the discharge of debt. However, a discharge may be denied, depending on the conduct of the debtor. Certain conduct by a debtor does not block a discharge of all debts but creates an exception to discharge as to a particular debt.

The discharge of a debtor is completely denied if the debtor has:

- Made any fraudulent transfers within one year before the filing of the petition.
- Made a false oath in connection with the bankruptcy case.
- Failed to explain satisfactorily any loss of assets or deficiency of assets to meet liabilities.
- Refused to obey any lawful order of the court (with certain exceptions relating to the invocation of the Fifth Amendment).

- Been granted a discharge within six years before the date of the filing of petition.

There are other grounds as well, and the banker and the lawyer should review all the grounds set forth in the Bankruptcy Code in detail to determine whether or not a discharge should be denied. If the bank decides to object to the discharge of the debtor, the complaint must be filed prior to the deadline set by the court.

Even if the debtor obtains a discharge, the discharge does not cover certain "nondischargeable" debts. These nondischargeable debts include such things as certain taxes and certain alimony payments. More important for the banker, however, is the provision which makes nondischargeable any debt for obtaining money, or an extension or refinance of credit by the use of a statement in writing that is materially false, respecting the debtor's (or an insider's) financial condition; that the debtor caused to be made or published with the intent to deceive, and on which the creditor reasonably relied.

Also, the code provides that a discharge will not discharge an individual debtor from any debt for obtaining money, or an extension or a refinancing of credit, by false pretenses or actual fraud, other than a false financial statement. An example might be false representations concerning the condition of collateral against which the bank extended credit.

Other debts which are not covered by a discharge include debts for fraud or defalcation while acting in a fiduciary capacity, embezzlement, or larceny; and for willful and malicious injury by the debtor to another entity or to the property of another entity.

There are some other exceptions, but they are not likely to be of particular interest to a bank in an ordinary situation.

As in the case of objecting to the grant of a discharge, an objection to the dischargeability of a particular debt must be filed by the deadline set by the court.

Index

4M 2/85
4M 7/85